Volume 15, Number 2
Spring 2014

Edited by Joe Mackall & Dan Lehman

Submissions

River Teeth invites submissions of creative nonfiction, including narrative reportage, essays, and memoirs, as well as critical essays that examine the emerging genre and that explore the impact of nonfiction narrative on the lives of its writers, subjects, and readers.

All articles must be submitted electronically via Submittable.

Visit www.riverteethjournal.com for instructions on submitting.

**Submissions will not be accepted May through August. **

River Teeth no longer accepts submissions through the mail. If you are unable to submit via Submittable, please contact the Managing Editor with your concern, Sarah Wells, riverteeth@ashland.edu or call (419)289-5957.

Subscriptions

River Teeth: A Journal of Nonfiction Narrative (ISSN 1544-1849) is published semiannually at $25 for individuals, $65 for institutions, and $16 for single issues by Ashland University. For subscriptions outside the United States, please add $16 for postage and handling. Make checks payable to *River Teeth* and mail to:

RIVER TEETH
Subscriptions
Ashland University
401 College Avenue
Ashland, OH 44805

Subscriptions may also be purchased using a credit card on our website. Visit www.riverteethjournal.com for more information.

Manufactured in the United States

Interior: Sarah M. Wells
Cover Design: Nicholas Fedorchak
Cover Photo: David FitzSimmons

Contents

Editor's Notes

Fifteen years into this journey, an important thing readers should know about *River Teeth* is that its two editors once worked at magazines and newspapers where we shaped content and nurtured writers. Hence our love for factual writing that soars in interesting ways. Beyond that, we love clustering great essays and literary reporting into the soul and rhythm of each issue. Though *River Teeth* is housed at a university and has been adopted as a reading text by nonfiction professors across the country, what we do here is much more than an academic exercise. We prowl for edgy, compelling nonfiction, crafting volumes that regularly make our readers take an extra breath and blink.

It's a high standard and difficult to define. Of course, sometimes we miss, but we do know what works when we see it and, thankfully, we hit the mark most of the time. Perhaps that's why, in the past year, we've had an essay recognized with a Pushcart, two pieces anthologized in *Best American Essays*, and five *BAE* notables. If you are counting (and we confess that we are), that's a record that simply no one else is matching—not even the long-running, deeply loved, commercial literary magazines that can pay writers much more and have been a traditional home for great American writing.

So how do we do it?

First of all, the two of us and the readers you see listed in the masthead peruse every one of the more than a thousand unsolicited manuscripts that come our way each year—even though we know we can accept only about ten or twelve of them. We root for each and every submission, hoping to find not only the perfect piece by a great writer whom we already love, but, as has happened, the fledgling writer whose first published piece will appear in *River Teeth* and will snare a Pushcart for the writer and for us.

Wait, you say, only ten or twelve unsolicited entries make the final cut? But don't we regularly publish at least twice that many nonfiction pieces each year? Where do the rest come from? Something here doesn't add up.

That's where we become magazine editors engaged in a never-ending search for whatever will make any issue the best it can be. Between us and our managing editor, we travel to conferences and workshops across the country. Frankly, some of the best of them are close to home: our own *River Teeth* Nonfiction Conference and the two-week annual intensives at our Ashland MFA. Top writers read from their work on these occasions, as they do at AWP, Nonfiction Now, and other places we hang out. If we hear something that is great, we go for it. Right then. We don't suffer a turn-down easily. Something about our enthusiasm for a piece, and about our vision for the journal and what we do, has convinced writers who otherwise don't owe us the time of day to take a shot with *River Teeth*. It's paid off for us, and they tell us it has paid off for them. A *River Teeth* publication means something important, as witness the contracts our writers sign and our results when winners are selected.

Beyond tracking down writers in person, all of us here prowl scores of websites like the *Nieman Storyboard* or *The Morning News* in search of great writing and writers who may be a fit for us. While we won't reprint essays or articles from major outlets, we will pick up a piece from a regional newspaper or magazine or an online zine that will help us shape an issue and introduce our readers to a great new voice who deserves to be heard. And, as we grow our base of subscribers and online library-access royalties, we now can commission new pieces from writers we love. The essay from our reigning Pushcart honoree Andre Dubus III—"Writing and Publishing a Memoir: What in the Hell Have I Done?"—was a commissioned piece. It was more than worth it for him and for us; we have many such new ideas percolating, and we welcome your suggestions.

At heart we always ask two questions: Is this the sort of piece I would want to call the other editor in the middle of the night to say we *have to have*? And would we die if we saw this piece in someone else's journal *and knew we could have had it for ourselves*? Those are the criteria, nothing else really. As we wrote a few issues ago, we will publish the work of friends and acquaintances (even ourselves) if it meets those standards. Only then. That's all. That our two *Best American* essays come from writers with close ties makes our case. Both were among the best dozen or so essays in this or any other year; it would have killed us to see them win those prizes for someone else. And we confessed that fact in writing before the prizes were won.

We know all this sounds more than a little intuitive, even presumptuous, and quite a bit less than arm's length. That's the nature of love, we guess.

Still, we probably owe you some articulated standard; heck, we owe it to ourselves. The best we've heard recently comes from Cheryl Strayed in her introduction to *Best American Essays 2013*. "Behind every good essay there's an author with a savage desire to know more about what is already known," she says. She reminds us all that great nonfiction writing is part philosophy, confession, recollection, reimagination, clarity, conjecture. Ultimately, she says, "the essay's engine is curiosity; its territory is the open road."

As for us, we're happy on that open road; we're glad you're with us for the ride.

—DWL

Water Rising

Leila Philip

Beavers are the Shiva of the animal world. Who knows how a beaver chooses where to make her pond? But once she does, trees fall like spears of light then overnight disappear, dragged to underwater lairs, or left to float eerie carcasses, every branch and shred of bark stripped clean.

Last week I saw the beaver who's been cutting down the woods near my house. It was evening, the weary light thinning through the trees by the time I reached the bridge. Sound came first, a crack so loud I flinched, thinking my neighbor had shot his gun. But across the newly flooded swamp, I saw a brown head cutting a silver *v*. Beaver, the first I'd seen.

One black eye visible, staring, back and forth she swam, a crease in flat silver, then she dove like some huge furious fish and her dark tail flicked up and slammed the surface. Another crack echoed through the trees, her warning.

Now my beaver swam faster and faster, back and forth before me on the bridge, fierce, her whole being focused on this one resolve, to make me go away. Again she slammed the water, sound booming through the trees.

This swamp was hers, her trickling dam, her fallen trees, her growing pond. Each day water rising. When I didn't move she began to track me, that dark eye locked on my standing figure.

And this time, when she dove, she took me with her, my svelte younger self moving through the hot water ladled with silt, down to the bottom of the pond where she had carved her underwater trails, clawing roads through the deep muck.

When I surfaced I was middle aged, messy in my ways as if I had grown four sets of yellow teeth, two layers of fur, claws, and dark scales cascading down the thick paddle tail. Half fish, but no mermaid.

Curious

Kim Todd

Flat head, lidless eyes, body dirt brown, the Surinam toad slithers through the pond like animated mud, an amphibian golem. Long fingers filter the swamp floor, sweeping fish and worms into a tongueless mouth. Some romantic gave it the alternate title "star-fingered toad," because after each foot divides into toes, the toes divide again, creating a "star" at the tip. But celestial the toads are not.

The most disturbing part, though, is the way they breed. Mating, they somersault through the water, the female dropping eggs on the male's belly when the pair is upside down. Turning, he brushes them onto her back and fertilizes. The eggs sink into her body, leaving pale warty bumps until, months later, fully formed miniature toads (not tadpoles) burst out and swim away. When they've gone, her back is all holes like a drained honeycomb.

In the seventeenth century, every collector in Amsterdam coveted a Surinam toad, in a box, in a painting, in a jar. The Dutch had colonized Surinam, a small country on the northeast shoulder of South America. Between planting sugar and pineapple, they marveled at the creations of the tropical rainforest. Frederik Ruysch, botanist and midwifery expert, kept one in his cabinet of curiosity, a gathering of oddities, the precursor to museums, where his friends could come gawk. Nicholaes Witsen, burgomaster and avid collector, reported seeing the disconcerting toad and described it: "all the back is open as a wound."

Some viewers interpreted the ugly appearance as a judgment for ugly habits: "The pipa is, in form, more hideous than even the common toad; nature seeming to have marked all these strange mannered animals with peculiar deformity," wrote Oliver Goldsmith in *A History of Earth and Animated Nature* in 1774.

Those who seek her out today still have a visceral response. Comments on a YouTube video of toadlets tearing the skin and kicking free include "damn nature you scary!" and "as a lover of animals im ashamed to say i said KILL it with fire and dont stop . . kill it burn it kill it burn it! then bury it and shoot the grave!" (A more sober-minded commenter suggested that, compared to watching a human birth, it wasn't bad at all.)

Given the strength of the recoil, why can't we look away? The YouTube video has been watched almost half a million times. Perhaps now you are tempted. Knowledge of South American toad habits has little practical application. What is the nature of the itch we call "curiosity"?

❖

Like the toad, curiosity is a strange beast. The investigating mind moves like a sleek little mammal, a mink maybe, rubbing up against things in the dark, trying to determine their shape, occasionally ripping with sharp teeth and pawing through the opening. Or perhaps a spider, creeping precisely, attaching silk here, and here, and here to impose a pattern where before was just air.

Curiosity can be as obsessive as hunger or lechery, swamping the senses. But it is notoriously fickle, too, slinking away as soon as it is satisfied. Its subjects seem so frivolous: a baby giraffe, a dodo skeleton, the Surinam toad. George Loewenstein, author of "The Psychology of Curiosity," summed it up: "The theoretical puzzle posed by curiosity is why people are so strongly attracted to information that, by the definition of curiosity, confers no extrinsic benefit." St. Augustine defined it is as "ocular lust," the desire to stare at an object, animal, or scene and let the mind roam. Charles Darwin, who you might think would value the trait, saw it as the enemy of substantive inquiry. He wrote in a letter to a friend: "Physiological experiment on animals is justifiable for real investigation, but not for mere damnable and detestable curiosity."

This kinship to physical passion—the strength of desire, the burst of delight—makes curiosity waver between vice and virtue. Intellectual curiosity sparks science, art, all kinds of innovation. Here, in most of twenty-first-century North America, it is held in the highest esteem. For much of history, though, coveting the secrets of the world and mulling over mushrooms and vipers threatened to drag one from thoughts of God. Religious and worldly contemplation were at odds. Thomas Brooks, an English nonconformist preacher of the early 1600s, warned, "Curiosity is the spiritual adultery of the soul. Curiosity is spiritual drunkenness."

Don't unlock the door. Don't open the box. Don't eat the apple. Fairy tales, Greek myths, and biblical stories caution against giving curiosity free rein. The warnings are dire. But so often, like Pandora, Eve, and Bluebeard's wife, we still extend our hand.

❖

In the late 1920s, Henry Nissen, a slight, bespectacled psychology graduate student at Columbia, took a more scientific approach to the question of the nature of curiosity. He noticed that white rats explored their cages, even if they had to delay eating or mating. How far would they go to satisfy their curiosity, he wondered? Nissen put male albinos in a cage linked to a passageway that would give the rats an electric shock when they crossed it. On the other side of the passageway, he created an irresistibly interesting environment for a rat (he hoped): a mini-maze of sheet-metal walls in a pine base, seeded with corks and piles of wood shavings and a rubber mat. The rats investigated, even at the price of pain.

Of course, this curiosity is not merely idle. It could be a life or death matter for a rat to know what lurks around an unfamiliar corner.

But for humans, it's more complex. Why, for example, might anyone want to read about rats shocking themselves in pursuit of wood shavings?

These questions intrigued Daniel Berlyne, working on his PhD in the 1940s at Yale. He distinguished between the exploring curiosity, shared with animals, and the kind he felt was uniquely human, "epistemic": that curiosity based in the desire for knowledge. What type of things triggered human curiosity, he wondered. What would be our equivalent to corks and a rubber mat? To find out, he gave undergraduates in the course "Normal Human Personality" at Brooklyn College a list of forty-eight questions about invertebrates.

For example:

"What crops do some ants cultivate in underground 'farms'?"

"What form does the clam's brain take?"

"How does the spider avoid being caught in its own web?"

"How do sea-wasps swim?"

Now, he said to them, and I say you, which makes you most curious?

Sifting through his results, Berlyne concluded that curiosity is spurred by the novel, the complex, the ambiguous, the uncertain, and the surprising. When elements previously thought of as incompatible are harnessed together—a juxtaposition—the curiosity grows stronger. Loewenstein described these traits as "violated expectations," and noted that, often, the closer the subject matter was to the observer's life, the more intense the need was to stare, to figure it out.

In a study published in 2009, scientist Min Jeong Kang and others recreated Berlyne's experiment using MRI equipment that let them see where blood flowed in the brain. They showed Cal Tech students slides with questions, then asked them to rate how curious they were about the answers. (The questions ranged farther afield than Berlyne's, covering rock bands, politics, and snack foods. It is worth noting, though, that one of the questions that prompted the most curiosity was "What is the only type of animal besides a human that can get a sunburn?" Animals make us endlessly curious.) These intellectual questions spurred a physiological response. Curious students' pupils dilated. Activity increased in the caudate nucleus, the bilateral prefrontal cortex, and the parahippocampal gyri, which the scientists interpreted as the brain anticipating a reward. Other studies have charted the way curiosity triggers the production and release of dopamine—a neurotransmitter associated with heightened arousal and motivation, creating the experience of pleasure. The mind becomes receptive, wakes up, that little mink grows hungry.

Incidentally, reading Berlyne made me realize how similar these traits are to what I ask of my writing students. The opening of their essays should make an irresistible offer to the reader—to show her that her assumptions about the way the world works are wrong, to present an odd juxtaposition and offer to unravel it, to reveal the strange hidden at the heart of the familiar. Not surprisingly, Berlyne later went on to study aesthetics, exploring what makes viewers stare at one painting longer, and with more pleasure, than another.

Given Berlyne's formulation, it makes sense that the Dutch couldn't stop looking at the Surinam toad. The animal, its life history, complicated questions they were asking about humans. For example, how did we breed? Some claimed they could see the man in miniature inside the sperm head. Others felt the egg contained the whole, a preformed creature that started to grow when nudged by the sperm. Still others argued for a more gradual development. And here was a swarm of tiny toads, emerging complete from their mother. It violated expectations of toad reproduction (eggs) and mammal reproduction (live birth). And from the mother's back? What could that mean? It was a disturbed mirror. Irresistible.

One of those most fascinated by the Surinam toad during Golden Age Amsterdam was an artist and naturalist named Maria Sibylla Merian. She was curious about metamorphosis—of insects, of frogs—and she visited the best Dutch cabinets of curiosity, including those of Ruysch and Witsen. But she was dissatisfied by what she found there. The preserved specimens didn't tell her how the creatures lived: what they ate, where they hid, how they moved from shape to shape.

So she went to Surinam to investigate, spending two years gathering plants and moths and lizards, raising them through their life cycles, taking notes. For her painting of the toad, she captured a female and dropped it in a jar of brandy as soon as the young broke the skin. In the final image, the Surinam toad is mid-eruption. The mother's face is impassive. One little toad swims behind her, ready to dart off into its own perverse life.

Several years ago, my own curiosity took me to Surinam. I was writing about Maria Sibylla Merian and her thirst to understand the insects, lizards, fruits, and toads of South America. I hoped to retrace her footsteps, wondering about her drive and self-conception. What was she doing there? How did she get away with it in a time when the slightest sign of eccentricity could cause someone to be burned as a witch? That a woman would travel to Surinam with her twenty-one-year-old daughter to conduct field studies three hundred years ago violated expectations. That strange juxtaposition of person and time and interest made me itch.

It was not an easy journey, for reasons both practical and emotional. The first airline where I bought a ticket went bankrupt a week before the plane left the ground, no one in Surinam answered my phone calls or emails as I tried to make arrangements, and I had to leave my nascent family—my husband and ten-month-old twins—for a week and a half. But this was my work; the money from this book was sustaining us, I told myself. Besides, I wanted to go. Chasing an epistemic question dilated my pupils, lit me on fire.

Despite my itchiness, though, I was not very brave. Not as brave as Cheryl, the anthropologist who hitchhiked on canoes into the rainforest to interview remote tribes of Maroons, descendants of escaped slaves who had fled the Dutch sugar plantations. She looked at the forest floor, found evidence of earlier ways of life. Cheryl said she'd arrange for me to fly to her study sites and I said no, afraid of her descriptions of the drug dealers and prostitutes and miners in the interior, of evenings spent picking ticks off each other over a sloth stew. Who knew what might happen? All I could picture was the tiny plane going down and my death in flames and broken branches.

Instead, I took the bus from the capital of Paramaribo to the National Zoological Collection of Suriname at Anton de Kom University. The university logo displays a Surinam toad next to a microscope. After a quick hard rain, steam rose off my clothes as the curator of invertebrates gave me the tour, highlighting the species that enthralled the Dutch: the lantern flies with heads reputed to light up, bat skeletons, hundreds of kinds of beetles. In a hallway packed with specimens, a Surinam toad glowed in a jar.

Leeched of color, floating in space, unmoored from time, the toad had transcended its lifespan with the help of pickling. She was less golem than ghost. The ragged holes left her looking mutilated. I could see that the attraction to her is snarled up in fear: dread of infestation and disfigurement, loss of bodily integrity.

Looking at the suspended skin and bone made me think for a moment, not about the toad, but about the jar. It's hard to analyze—a form of dissection—subjects in motion. How much easier to go part by part when they are held still. Think of where we put our curiosities: in a bottle, in a zoo, in a glass display case with their stuffed peers. Faced with an object in isolation, the mind can stretch its muscles, crawl and explore. The blank background forces focus, a situation that we crave, but that is ultimately artificial, stripped of vital information.

❖

The image of the pale toad in the jar makes me think of Barbara Benedict's recent book *Curiosity: A Cultural History of Early Modern Inquiry*. She traces the evolution of curiosity during the seventeenth and eighteenth centuries in Europe, the era of Maria Sibylla Merian and many other curious folks. This period included the scientific revolution, Linnaeus's categorization, comprehensive exploration of the Americas, the birth of the novel. Even as curiosity gained respect, though, it remained suspect in women particularly, a category that includes Eve, Bluebeard's wife, and Pandora, as well as gossips, women thrilling with useless information. The reason? As Benedict says: "Curiosity is the mark of discontent" and "curiosity is seeing your way out of your place." One of the things that makes us most curious is the suggestion that the world isn't how we think it is, that our categories are the wrong ones, and the promise is that the answer to our questions will give us a different, fuller, better, view.

It's easy to dismiss this criticism as reflecting another world, one more obsessed with maintaining the status quo and keeping women in their place. But Benedict makes other points, too, about the nature of curiosity, points that are harder to ignore. The way, for example, that items in the cabinets of curiosity (and modern-day museums and zoos) have been stripped of their use, of their ability to work. A bow and arrow, a ceremonial mask—to be a curiosity, they have to become not a way to feed yourself or talk with the gods but an artifact. To own one means you have the status to possess a bow and arrow for decorative purposes. Curiosity can turn the objects of its desire into, well, objects. They can enter the system of commerce; they can be used and then discarded. Bluebeard, Benedict reminds us, was also curious. He had his own collection—of women's heads, which he could study without having to contemplate their subjectivity, their humanity.

❖

Before I left to go to Surinam, the toad seemed to be a story about ocular lust and the extent people will go to satisfy it. But it's also a story about the glass, its insulating properties, the attraction of those boundaries. They keep us safe—not just safe to make precise observations, but also safe from being observed ourselves. Maybe this is the real danger of curiosity, the teeth in the warning. Thought it's easy to laugh at Brooks, the preacher who claimed "curiosity is spiritual drunkenness," maybe he has a point about the risk that it will distort our sense of what is important, that it will obscure the big picture.

For curiosity to have value, perhaps we have to allow it to be the beginning of something larger, to pursue it past the initial itch, the spark of hunger, the quick answer, the dopamine burst, to the "real investigation" Darwin asked for. Darwin, so hard on curiosity, was relentless at looking at the big picture, of looking at creatures through time, of challenging categories, and turning the mirror back on humans. We have to see the disturbed world it implies, and ourselves living within it, moving beyond the role of observer, of questioning mind.

Several days after seeing the toad in the jar, I paced along one of the trails through the Brownsberg Nature Park, at the edge of the rainforest, through the tall trees with invisible crowns, the wasps building bulbous nests on the branches, the odd smashed fruit spilling its seeds in the dust. The plants Merian picked and painted often didn't have European names—she worked with the head of Amsterdam's botanical gardens to categorize them—but in places she used the Amerindian name or left the plant nameless. Brown-furred flanks rustled in the bushes. Monkey tails unfurled into upside-down question marks.

Maybe my question about Merian was never going to have a definitive answer. Certainly, I could never know what was going on in her mind. Maybe the question was going to change as I pursued it. Certainly, its pursuit was changing me.

Off to the side of the trail, a mud-colored head poked out of a small pond. I knelt to see if it was a Surinam toad, but with half its body submerged, no real line between skin and water, I couldn't say. No label declared it rare or important or special or forbidden. No brandy or videotape scissored it from time. It had escaped the box, like one of Pandora's demons, and now might breed or rot or pioneer some new behavior, do its work of living, participating in the fleshlife of the forest. And for the moment, I was content not to know. Anything could happen. And then it ducked back under, out of reach.

❖

Answers (just in case you were curious):

Ants cultivate edible fungus in underground "farms." Interestingly, the seventeenth-century Dutch generally and Merian specifically were also fascinated by these same ants, the leaf cutter ants of Central and South America. They scissor bits of leaves and carry them over their heads like green sails back to the anthill. Early naturalists proposed many theories for what the ant was doing—using the leaves as food or miniature roofs—but it would take a nineteenth-century biologist unravel the mystery.

The clam doesn't have what we would recognize as a brain. It has three "nerve centers," pairs of ganglia near the mouth, near the foot, and near the back of the body.

A spider doesn't stick to its own web because only some threads of the web are sticky, and the spider avoids them. In addition, its legs are covered with a nonstick coating, and specialized claws allow it to move lightly and precisely.

Despite a fascinating life history presented to the undergraduates by Berlyne in an effort to spur their interest, the nine-inch-long sea-wasp, a creature with a fatal sting whose main enemy is the sea-wasp-eating porpoise, is fictional.

And, finally, the correct answer in the Cal Tech study was "pigs sunburn." More recent research has shown that whales sunburn, too.

On Kids and Bombs
(or How To Be a Hummingbird)

Steven Church

Providence, Rhode Island, 2005. The rain had been coming down in sheets for nine days straight. Seriously. Seeping through the walls in our basement, leaving puddles beneath the oil tank. We needed to get out of the house and we drove fast, just barely tethered to the asphalt, headed for a movie in Massachusetts, a movie about a giant were-rabbit ravaging the village gardens. The red and green and yellow lights flowered in the moist fog. They twinkled and blinked intermittently with green. It was too much sometimes, too heavy. This place. This moment in time. The white noise of water spray competed with the radio voices. Our three-year-old son blithely chattered away in his car seat, conversing with his invisible friend, Tum-Tum the elephant.

Meanwhile my wife and I talked openly about recent bomb threats to subways in New York City. We said whatever we wanted—things like, "bound to happen," and "nothing we can do," or "just gets worse and worse." We admitted that this was our reality now. But a claymation movie about a giant were-rabbit awaited us, and we were happy about this. We were out of the house and not thinking, just driving and living. We were good Americans. It was early October, 2005, and we'd already decided not to go to New York before the bomb threats were issued—mainly because we couldn't afford the trip. But when we'd heard the reports of threats to subways and public transit, we were both honestly relieved to be anywhere but the city.

"Can you imagine that?" she asked, responding to another NPR update on the car radio.

"Getting bombed?" I asked.

"Yeah," she said. "Or living with that threat every day like they do in so many other places."

"No, no. I can't imagine."

I suddenly realized that our son had gone silent; and the moment began to stretch and expand, distended with silence. He was listening to everything we'd said. He was paying attention to all the words and possibilities, looking for the suggestion of violence or fear or conflict because he had Doppler radar for such drama.

"Who's getting bombed, Daddy?" he asked.

"Nobody, honey," my wife said, "Daddy and Mommy were just talking."

"It's a figure of speech," I chimed in, but I was kidding myself.

He understood. He listened to NPR every morning and heard me ranting at the voices. I didn't want him to be afraid of war and bombs. I didn't want him to feel targeted. I wanted him to stay young and innocent and fearless as long as possible. But I also didn't want to shelter him from the truth or from real danger. I had to prepare him to live in a world where people bombed trains or sporting events or buildings. But how was I supposed to do this? I was in the midst of a full-on parental pause, a seizure of language, and I didn't know what to say.

Then my wife swooped in: "What do you want to be when you grow up?"

He paused for a moment, letting the possibilities balloon.

"Hmmmm," he said, "maybe a hummingbird."

A hummingbird.

I'd clearly underestimated our son's capacity for hope and dreams of the future. He wanted to be a hummingbird and wasn't it my job to make that happen?

❖

Fresno, California, April 15, 2013. My son the hummingbird, born almost nine months after 9/11, will soon turn eleven. He's just a few years older than Martin Richard, the youngest victim of the 2013 Boston Marathon bombing. My son is a bright boy who takes painting lessons, plays the trombone, and dreams of being a filmmaker. He still likes birds but he doesn't want to be one when he grows up.

His mother now has a house a few blocks away from me. My son and his sister live with me half of every week. Things have changed a lot in eight years. Our understanding of family and home has changed. But my son tells me that he still likes listening to NPR in the car because he learns cool things. These days he's been listening to the news of the Boston Marathon bombing, not far from where we used to live, and the subsequent manhunt with what appears to be a kind of careful detachment, a calculated preadolescent disinterest. But he knows all the details, knows the bombs were packed in pressure cookers, knows they blew peoples' legs apart, and he knows the bombs killed a young boy.

My five-year-old daughter seems mostly oblivious to the news; she makes up songs in the back seat as we drive from school to home and listen to the radio reports. She doesn't ask the same questions that my son asked years before, but I know from experience that she's listening. I know she's absorbing it all. She doesn't miss a thing. And I suppose that's what I'm reminded of every time something like this happens. Such things have the capacity to shrink your reality down to what really matters, making the world seem tiny and impenetrable, while simultaneously expanding things exponentially until your world seems immense and fragile and impossible to maintain.

I was still a new parent when my son first became aware of bombs, when he first started to ask "why" questions about war and violence. I can't say that I know a lot more now than I did then. But perhaps *he* knew something then that we can all try to remember.

He knew that he wanted to be a hummingbird.

He may have been small but he thought big and wild and in ways I aspired to match, ways that I still hope to preserve in my daughter and myself. If I could I'd take them both out in the yard the next time a bomb or some other violence tears through the fabric of our days. Just the three of us. Our faces pressed up close to the flowers, and I'd tell them how to do it, tell them to remember the nectar, remember their wings, their imaginations, and the way they can beat against the pull. It's a simple matter of defying gravity. I want to free them and protect them with this one fact: a hummingbird can beat its wings seventy times in one second. A simple blur of breath and flesh and they could be gone.

Fish

Marley Andino

I.

I locked up my cinderblock cottage and drove straight east from New Mexico, outrunning a December snowstorm coming off the Sangre de Cristo Range. Two days later, when I coasted bleary over the Virginia border and saw the familiar line of haze and mountains, I felt something like yearning. I was twenty-three, and hadn't seen Mom—or anyone else—in two years.

Mom's house was quiet when I pulled up. I stood in the driveway, looking at the three stories of ugly salmon brick, at the salt-stained concrete path, at the front door with its clash of red paint. I wondered who I'd find—Mom had a fondness for drifters.

I walked the puzzle of rooms, calling out. The huge house was closeted and dim, and felt older than it really was. My old bedroom on the third floor had been relegated to tenants long ago, and over the years every inch of the house had been torn down and reconfigured: doors moved, windows blocked, walls added. She'd covered the solid walnut floors with carpet remnants and throw rugs. "All that dark wood is depressing," she always said.

I hadn't told anyone I was coming. I discovered my little sister,

Jasmine, reading in her airless bedroom, the heavy drapes over the bay window pulled back to show Mom's never-finished reglazing project. A ladder leaned against the glass outside, in the same position as two years before.

"You're back!" Jasmine shrieked. She jumped up to hug me. "You're back!"

I hugged her and inhaled her smell—not soap, or perfume, just good kid sweat. "For a few days. I wanted to surprise you guys . . . Where is everyone?" I stood back and looked at her—she was almost twelve, taller than last time, but still too thin.

"Edward and Mom went to town."

Edward, my ex-boyfriend from high school, was still living with Mom. Last time I visited, Mom told me she'd put the house in his name, just to make sure us kids didn't fight over it when she died. I didn't care much about Edward and Mom, but I was anxious to see my little brother.

"Joey went too?" I asked.

"Joey doesn't live here," Jasmine said. She looked at me with big eyes, mouth turned up at the edges in a permanent little joker smile.

"What do you mean?"

"He lives in a big house downtown with some other kids. I got to visit him there and they have a game room, and a bunch of bicycles. He can just pick one and ride it anywhere."

It wasn't the first time Mom had sent Joey away, but it was still a surprise. I went to the hall and peeked inside Joey's room. It didn't look like a thirteen-year-old's bedroom—it was a mess of overstuffed fruit crates from the health-food store where Mom worked, and stacks of unopened mail. I picked up a handful of papers and snooped through them. There were bills from Joey's psychiatrist. He'd been going since he was six, ever since he got violent. Joey was the canary in our family—only instead of keeling over, he put up a fight to show us something was wrong.

I laid the bills down just as I'd found them. I waited around for a while for Mom, and when she didn't come, Jasmine and I drove a half-mile to the country store for hot cocoa.

When we got back home with our cocoa, Mom was sitting at the sticky kitchen table with a Mason jar of coffee. She sat formally, dressed as usual in neatly patched jeans and an old man's button down— "chore clothes," she called them. Her curly hair was still dark brown. I could tell she'd cut it herself again, wings of uncooperative hair sticking out from behind each ear.

Mom looked up at me and smiled.

I didn't waste time saying hello. "Where's Joey?"

"He's where he needs to be," Mom said. She pushed back her coffee and stood up. "I've got things to do, for Christmas." She walked towards the door, where the sign Edward swiped from our high school auditorium was still nailed up: *Entrance A and Exit A.*

I watched her through the kitchen window as she disappeared into the back woods. I knew what she was doing. In the old days, when my father was still around, we'd drive all over town looking for a live Christmas tree with a root ball. "It's a shame to kill a perfectly good tree," Mom always said. Most years the tree stayed up, withered and brown in a corner of the living room, until March, or sometimes April. She insisted on buying a nice white pine year after year, even though we all knew it was destined to die. After Dad left, the trees got skinnier, and for the last seven or eight years she'd go out back to gather branches, "fresh-cut boughs," she said, so she could make her own tree.

Jasmine and I sat alone in the kitchen, sipping cocoa. I studied her face: translucent blue under her eyes, long, fine lashes. I felt a sudden protectiveness as I remembered her, not so long ago, as a baby. I'd visited her in the glass room at the hospital, right after she was born. I didn't hold her but stood there with Dad's sister looking into the sealed bassinet. For some reason I started to cry for this small person attached to wires, respirator pumping air into collapsed lungs. "I don't want her to die," I said, and my aunt took my hand. Two weeks later, when Jasmine came home from the hospital, a crib replaced the big oak desk in the corner of my bedroom. I stood over her, fascinated by the perfection of her miniature lips as she slept, as if sealed by wax. I remembered how, in a moment of boredom, I'd softly pinched her nostrils together. How she'd struggled for a moment and then the wax seal popped open with a satisfying *aah*.

"You hungry?" I asked Jasmine. "I'll make pancakes."

"Nah."

We sat at the kitchen table, and she looked over at me with her half-smile, fidgeting, like she wanted to tell me something.

"What?" I said.

"I know what rape is."

I heard the words, but didn't know what to think. Jasmine's expression didn't change. I sat there, waiting.

She started to tell me—like she was talking about homework or what to have for dinner—what one of Mom's boarders had done to her during the years he'd lived up on the third floor. Mom had liked Wayne. He was part Cherokee, she'd said. She overlooked the fact he had no job, no way to pay rent. He'd moved out long ago, but I remembered him—hated him—for axing up my brother's favorite oak tree and spray-painting his fat initials under my sister's window.

Jasmine spoke in monotone, sometimes looking up at me. She didn't seem to know how bad it was, what she was telling me. I held her hand, rubbing the stubs of her chewed-down fingernails. "I'm sorry," I said. "I'm so sorry." I didn't want to scare her by crying, so I hugged her, played with her long hair, distracted her by telling stories of the New Mexico desert, of coyotes and canyons.

An hour later, Mom came inside with an armload of boughs. I followed her to the living room, where she sat on the floor, making her tree, tying the boughs together with bag-ties she'd saved from loaves of bread.

"Jasmine told me something awful, Mom, something horrible." She didn't look up, but I went on. "Wayne—he raped her, back when he lived here."

Mom kept twisting bag ties around the sappy branches.

"Mom, it wasn't once, it was for two years. We've got to do something, call the police."

Mom shook her head no. "If anything happened—you know your sister's imagination—it was ages ago. It would be hard to bring it back up. Besides, who even knows where Wayne is these days?"

"I'll do something, if you won't." I'd stood up to her a few times before, and it usually ended with her throwing my stuff out on the front walk, or telling me not to show my face around her place. I waited for her reaction, but she went on tying her boughs.

I wasn't going to cry, or let Mom see how desperate I felt. She didn't stop me when I picked up the phone and called the rape crisis number in the front of the phonebook, or when I wrote down the name of someone Jasmine could talk to.

That night, we ate dinner together—Jasmine, Mom, Edward, and I—at a table set with candles, like the world wasn't caving in. Edward sat quiet and gangly in a captain's chair at the head of the table, hair redder than I remembered. Mom served his plate and then passed the food down to Jasmine and me. Edward had gone vegan, and Mom's casserole was a gritty concoction of raw kale and spelt she'd adapted from *Let's Have Healthy Children*.

Before I drove back to New Mexico, I knocked on Jasmine's bedroom door and found her sitting in the middle of her unmade bed.

"Jasmine? I'm leaving, but I'll be back. Promise. We'll have fun next Christmas, huh?"

Jasmine didn't say anything, just gave me her charming half-smile. I handed her my old copy of *Our Bodies, Ourselves* from the attic.

"Mom doesn't really like to talk about this stuff. It's all here, though."

"Okay."

"Hey, Monday you're going to see a lady who can help you. You can talk to her about anything, about what you told me. She won't tell Mom."

I hugged her tight and felt like a traitor for leaving.

That night I slept in the room beside her, and had my same, stupid dream again. I'm leaving for somewhere and I'm packing and cleaning and the more I clean the more dirt I see, underneath, hidden, like painted-over wallpaper that looks good on the outside but hides something rotten.

When I called two weeks later to check on things, Mom said Jasmine sat mute through four or five sessions, until the therapist said she was wasting her time.

II.

Out in New Mexico, I could barely concentrate on my university studies. I'd call from the payphone down on the plaza, and Jasmine would tell me about Joey moving in and out of the Youth Attention Home downtown, or funny stories about Mom's new boarders. But she clammed up about Cherokee Wayne. I figured she was one of those kids who blocks trauma out, to make it seem like nothing ever happened. I didn't want to be the one to make it real.

It was fall before I had the nerve to visit Mom's brother down in Albuquerque, to tell him I was worried about the kids. I told him about Wayne, and Joey moving around, about the drifters coming and going. I was hoping he'd say it was Mom's job to make sure the kids were safe, that I couldn't spend my life worrying about something I couldn't control. "Why don't you go back?" my uncle said. "Try to change things."

The summer after graduation, I moved back east into a farmhouse in the Shenandoah Valley, an hour north of Mom's. I told everyone it was for grad school—and that was true—but it was mostly so I could be closer to Jasmine and Joey.

The red farmhouse was built into the side of a hill, fifty feet away from a natural spring that rose out of the ground in a curious, bubbling swell. It fed a series of wooden trout pools built up around the house, all connected by a rickety mess of wooden walkways. Smaller pools continued into the stone cellar of the house, where the young fry spent their first few weeks before being moved outdoors with the older trout.

I was the new night caretaker, there to make sure the oxygen pumps stayed on, droning and churning, keeping the fish alive. I'd go to graduate school during the day and listen for the alarm at night and on weekends. When I'd applied for the job, the owner showed me around the property, walking me behind the filet house to a bank of rusty pumps. "Trout are just like us," he said. "Eight minutes without oxygen, and they're dead."

The previous caretaker had planted a garden on the hill behind the house, and the tomatoes and zucchini were just ripening when Jasmine came to spend the weekend. We were out in the garden, Jasmine and I, picking yellow tomatoes shaped like tiny, perfect pears, when she turned towards me like she was near bursting.

"Can you keep a secret?" she asked.

I was good with secrets.

"I'm in love. You can't tell anybody. . . . It's Henry."

"Buck's friend, Henry? Come on—he's got to be at least twenty." Henry and our older brother, Buck, were best friends; he practically lived at Mom's.

"Twenty-two," Jasmine corrected me.

I looked at Jasmine. Her hand-me-down jeans hung loose on her frame, and her long hair was tucked into a dark, unbrushed ponytail. Something about her looked old for thirteen.

"You won't tell, will you?" she said, grinning.

"No," I said, "I won't tell."

We kept picking the tomatoes, and suddenly the sun was too hot and I felt nauseated. We went inside but the house was stifling. I tugged at the painted-shut windows, craving air, but they didn't budge, and when Jasmine asked if I was okay, I didn't answer.

The next morning we woke up early and made scrambled eggs for breakfast. Jasmine helped me feed the trout. We stood together on the wooden gangway, and I scattered the feed, and the trout jumped in anticipation and gobbled the tiny pellets in midair. A wild kitten that was always slinking around the grounds stood in the shadows of the tanks, watching, hoping for a stray fish.

I hadn't slept well, thinking of what Jasmine had told me, but I was probably reading too much into it. It couldn't be what I feared—it was just a crush.

I let Jasmine throw a scoop, and the fish leapt up again in a seething mass.

"Tell me about Henry," I said. I knew she trusted me.

"We're serious, if that's what you mean." She threw another scoop into the air. "We just had our two-year-and-three-month anniversary. We're careful. I won't get pregnant. Henry says people will want to break us up if they know about us."

I did the math: She'd been eleven when it started. They'd been together when I visited the year before, at Christmas. I hadn't seen it. I hadn't stopped it. A familiar tightness seeped into my gut. I wanted to hold her, but just stood there, not knowing what to do.

That evening Jasmine and I made dinner together, stripping the innards from the zucchini and stuffing them with breadcrumbs, chopped cherry tomatoes, and lemon basil. I felt like it was my own heart breaking when I told her that, sometimes, what feels like love is the good feeling you get from attention.

Later that night, I called Buck.

Jasmine pleaded by the phone. "I hate you," she cried, "I'll never forgive you."

But her secret weighed on me, and I'd spent too much time being quiet.

Buck drove Mom the hour north to the farmhouse for a family meeting. When things got crazy, one of us would call a meeting and we'd hash it out. We'd had a few secret meetings, too—without Mom—but she always suspected and complained that we were plotting to have her committed.

This meeting was no secret. Jasmine sat with us outside on the deck overlooking the pools, in the shade of the bitter hops that overran the trellis.

Mom said it wasn't a crime. Jasmine should have listened to her warnings that boys were trouble. Buck wanted to find Henry and hurt him—bad. I suggested letting the law take care of things.

No amount of explaining could convince Jasmine that Henry was wrong and we had to do something.

"Leave Henry alone. I love him." Her eyes were swollen. "If you want to go after someone, get Wayne."

Everyone went quiet and the drone of the oxygen pumps seemed too loud.

"I'll tell them everything," she said. "I remember."

She had stopped crying and looked strangely detached, feet tucked up on the long wooden bench, arms locked around her knees. "Wayne is the one who should be in trouble, not Henry. I'll tell the police everything. If you leave Henry out of it."

She had offered up something I couldn't resist, the chance to make something—one thing—right. Buck called Henry, demanded he leave town and never contact Jasmine again. Then I dialed the police. I told them everything I knew about Cherokee Wayne.

III.

I made long drives to the city. I sat inside the room where Jasmine and the detectives gathered around a tape recorder, holding her hand. But when it was time to go over the statements, I left her. A stronger person might have been able to hear the story, every detail—but I couldn't. I stood outside the soundproof door, forehead against the cool glass, waiting.

By the end of summer, the red farmhouse was suffocating. Inside, it smelled of the young trout in the basement, and outside the water bubbled up from the spring stinking like fertilizer from the farms in the valley.

The fish died. All of them. I heard the alarm and called the owners and we ran out, Jasmine and I. We stood around the huge wooden tanks and scooped out dead fish as they floated to the top. We aerated, with flailing arms beating the water, and more fish floated up, and soon it was an unstoppable tide of belly-up trout. We climbed into the chest deep pools, frantic, the owners yelling "Pull them out, get them out!" and we threw fish out as fast as we could, trying to make room for the living fish to breathe.

"Someone turn off that damn alarm," one of the owners screamed.

After an hour, we stood useless, sweating, knee deep in slime and death, and I started to cry. The wild kitten came out of hiding and gnawed on the broken, stinking fish.

* *The names in this piece have been changed for privacy.*

What I Learned from a Cockfighter

Christopher Bundy

Feel like a fighting rooster—feel better than I ever felt.

–Bob Dylan, "Cry Awhile"

Hundreds of crowing cocks broadcast their territory in a never-ending loop of five notes. A concert of noise that will either drive you mad or set you smiling at nature's harmonies. And the birds, feathers glistening like bourbon in a glass, black and red and orange, the colors of scandal and sin. They waltz as far as their tethers will allow, their beady bird eyes watching me sideways. I'm out of my element, a city kid in the country, and I step lightly.

From the interior Sandhills just east of Columbia to the Atlantic coast, the South Carolina Lowcountry is built on the remnants of ancient Miocene dunes that have left the soil sandy. Towards the coast, the land flattens along the Lowcountry Highway. As you drive through small towns like Yemassee, with its remnants of Civil War–era fortifications and evidence of recent commercial growth, the air dampens and richens. From there it's on to the narrow two-lane US 17 and its canopy of live oaks dripping with hoary tufts of Spanish moss. Roadside melon and tomato stands, maybe some boiled peanuts too, lead you to tidal marshes and finally the Atlantic, where the salty air hits you full on.

I haven't seen my old friend MD for ten years but he feels familiar as family. He strokes his mustache, adjusts his stained and faded baseball cap (*Corona*), spreads his tree-trunk arms before him, and says, "My babies." MD owns a cock farm, raising some of his roosters to fight on the Southeastern cockfighting circuit. There are over a hundred roosters enclosed in a large fenced yard next to his modest mobile home. He owns five hundred acres near the Edisto River, inherited when his father died, and leases much of the land to tenants, farmers, and the forest service. This is MD's kind of place—isolated, wild, and financially productive. It's how he makes his living. But he also makes money off of his birds—while he breeds some of them, others are gamecocks.

A sacred animal to many, the rooster has long been a symbol of power and pride, vigilance and bravery, masculinity and mortality. The double entendre we giggle at exists in other languages as well, the cock a measure of the man. But that's no joke. When you see a rooster crowing and clucking, waltzing the yard, its neck extended and its head high, you see its majesty, its royal comb and bulldog-like wattle, the arrogance and authority we've imposed on this fancy-feathered chicken. A beautiful animal. But the rooster is no cuddly pet, no puppy or kitten. It is an animal that will instinctively beat trespassing roosters to death. It is life and death.

According to the Humane Society, "in a cockfight, two roosters fight each other to the death while people place bets. Cockfighters let the birds suffer untreated injuries or throw the birds away like trash afterwards. Besides being cruel, cockfighting often goes hand in hand with gambling, drug dealing, illegal gun sales and murder." Cockfighting is among the most ancient of sport. Many suppose it began with the rise of ancient Persian and Indian societies; even then it was a spectator sport linked with gambling. Humans domesticated the fowl and pitted cock against cock even before we took to eating the meat and eggs of the hen. The death match came first. The Greeks adopted the sport; the Romans too. The Chinese and the sons of Israel. The Buddhists and the Hindus, Christians and Muslims. The Africans, Europeans, and Southeast Asians. Later the West Indians and the Americans, north, central, and south.

I knew that MD had been into cockfighting for years, but I don't see him much and didn't know how serious he'd become as a "cocker." I'd never seen him fight a gamecock, an insider and illegal event. Yet it was not hard to imagine my old friend slinging a bloodied and lifeless rooster into a fire pit behind his mobile home. In the past, MD and I had disagreed over beers about the ethics of what is commonly called a blood sport. As a good liberal I felt certain the issue was black and white, and that I had the moral leg up. I'm not a pet person—no dogs or cats or bunnies in my house, not even pretty birds or a quiet fish or a turtle in a tank. I don't like zoos and aquariums, and I don't hunt. I don't mind eating animals, as long as I don't have to see how they live and die. But I don't abide those who abuse animals; I believe we should generally leave them be. Putting two birds in a closed ring and relying on their natural instincts in order that one animal will kill the other ain't right. It makes compelling sport and money for some, but it ain't right.

I knew he'd dabbled in the sport, like a hobby, but he was now into raising champion cocks on his farm. At fifty-five my old friend had gone pro. But drug dealing? Selling assault rifles out of the trunk of his Toyota? No. A small crop of marijuana, maybe, and for personal use only, and a shotgun or deer rifle traded here and there over beers on someone's back porch. I recall snapshots of roosters in his yard, mysterious weekends away, hints of another life, but never chose to really see. Nor did he offer particulars, always keeping the most intimate details of his life close. To me MD has always been invulnerable and wise—hulking, with hands like hammers, but a gentle soul who understands the difference between right and wrong. And because we came from such disparate worlds—me, a suburban kid who went to college and labors occasionally on weekends, planting an annual or edging a lawn; him, a Lowcountry farm boy who never went to college and has labored most of his life. I trust his understanding of the natural world. Who let me hold my first and only alligator? Who taught me not to fear what feared me more? Took me out in a boat tossed by Atlantic waves the night after drinking too much Beam and taught me how to throw a net for shrimp? Demonstrated how to dig a ditch and not kill yourself doing it (because ditch digging will kill you)? Showed me that nobody should be too proud to pick up trash or clean a toilet? Proved that you could get what you want and still be nice to people? That you didn't have to like them, but you could be nice to them. I'm still a nature wuss, but intellectually I understand the need to both respect and embrace the natural world, despite its seemingly perpetual desire to kill me, or at least fuck me up a little.

Dozens of roosters strut as far as their tethers allow around blue barrels turned upside down, each with a tiny doorway cut into them, shade huts for the roosters like a cookie-cutter suburban development lined up in neat rows. A bowl of water sits beside each barrel. The roosters crow and crow, endlessly. It's a myth that they only crow at dawn. They crow all goddamn day. But I like the sound, the racket soothing me, and I turn on my digital recorder to capture the craziness. It's a sound I find exotic under the circumstances. There is romance in the noise, the blast of nature. I am excited by and curious about the scene because I just don't see shit like this in the city. I see curious things but not this.

MD is proud of his birds and eager to show me around. When I express an interest, he talks even more, revealing a conviction beyond financial reward that I have trouble understanding. Or maybe I understand the sort of philosophical conviction better than I do the one in which he's purely in it for the money, which seems opportunistic, benefiting from the destruction of another, even if that other is a bird. A natural-order sort of rationale. For the moment, I try to see what he sees.

MD gives me a quick tour of the farm, roosters scurrying as we walk by, their feathers glistening in the noon sun. I've never seen anything like it outside of a petting zoo (city kid): animals everywhere, including hens and chicks in abundance, a flock of sheep, several piglets, and a pack of dirty dogs in all sizes and (mixed) breeds pacing the outside of the fence, both shepherd and predator, of which I'll see evidence later.

The South Carolina Lowcountry spans from the lower midlands all the way to the coastal plains. This part of the world is a special place for me. Mostly because I have invented a deeper past and relationship with the Lowcountry than I can really claim. I try to visit once a year and I know the various beaches and tourist attractions. I can speak imaginatively and romantically of the coastline. Much of my mother's family is from nearby and has been for over three hundred years. I spent part of my summers swimming in the black waters of the Edisto, like my mother did when she was a child, and her mother and father before her, and probably further back, something I should know but don't because I've never bothered to read what is written about my family. Something I'd like to correct. I can't even understand why I haven't but I haven't. Laziness, probably—even that reasoning lazy. Instead I imagine I have history here, though I don't really know what it is. I have to make up a past that is no more romantic and compelling than the real thing. I just don't know the real thing. My link to this sandy soil relies not on actual roots but an invented mythology—or a pastiche of the selective history I do know, or at least think I know, no longer sure which is mythology and which is history.

I spent one charmed summer on a barrier island near Beaufort, South Carolina, as a young man on my own. I worked in the sun by day and drank beer under the stars by night as the ocean rolled before my girlfriend and me, whoever she was then. I, a recent reader of Thoreau, aimed for simple living and self-sufficiency, that was my plan, driven by both the austerity and the wildness, wanting both, getting mostly wildness, though you could certainly not call my life then complicated. It has never been so simple. But I was reckless, indestructibly stupid—a gift primarily of the young and curious. And I met MD, like a young uncle who had returned from great adventures full of knowledge. At six foot seven, he towered over even my tall frame. His bushy mustache and ever-present Wayfarers made him look like Magnum, P.I., which in 1987 was very cool. When he spoke, you believed he'd already known the wider world. In fact, he was barely thirty years old, recently a father and divorced, and had hardly left the state his whole life. Married young out of love or obligation, I don't know, as that part of his life, like many others, was already placed out of reach and rarely discussed.

But I never bothered to learn more about him. I was as self-absorbed as I've ever been. So I romanticized him then, and do so now, without ever really understanding him. We're old friends, something special and probably tied only to that summer on an island working together in the sand and dirt. But I don't know five verifiable things about him.

I return to the Lowcountry whenever I can to see the ocean, smell the briny air, and walk the sandy soil beneath palmetto trees and Spanish moss in the scenic marshlands. There is romance here, of a time and a place and a person I'll never be again. Others have described the South Carolina coast better than I can. But I like the *idea* of being from this region—and have said so, that I am from the "Lowcountry" more than once—even if I'm not really. When I'm there I feel at home, though I'm not. I feel and strut like a local who doesn't care for tourists, though I'm not one but the other. I feel like I'm adventuring when I'm only a few hours from home. But what I saw this time on my old friend's farm was the disarray of small, impoverished Southern towns, a stereotype: a truck on cinderblocks, a massive bolted shipping container with *Evergreen* on the side parked like an eighteen-wheeler and holding a mystery, various rusting and forgotten tools, an abandoned ATV, tires (always tires), hens and chicks scurrying around the weedy yard, and his dogs lying lazily in the shade of a scrub pine. This doesn't surprise me. MD has always lived like this, like a country boy. And he is one. He doesn't mind the disorder or the dirt that comes from living close to the land. He doesn't mind that nature doesn't give a shit about us, yet he gives a shit about nature. A guarded man who respects his environment but will kick it in the shins when he has to, just because that's the way of it. We're very different.

As I step lightly to avoid sheep and dog shit, MD scoops one of the roosters off the ground and holds it before me, a handsome bird whose feathers glisten (there really isn't a better verb for what these feathers do) in the sun. Because the birds are bred to fight, the comb and wattle (the red bits on top of their head and under their beaks) have been removed, as they can be detrimental in a bout. Again, I'm not an animal guy, so arm's length is as close as I want to get to a fighting cock. But MD insists I hold my arm out, palm up. With his looming frame—he actually blocks out the sun in the sky as he towers over me—he's convincing. But it's more than that. I don't want to be chickenshit in front of my old friend. While MD has always forgiven me my wussiness, it's a matter of pride. He already knows I'm a nature wimp, but he's never said anything. He just grabbed a rattlesnake by the head or handed me a baby gator. Or peeled a deer from my front fender and said, "There's fifty pounds of deer meat here, perfessor." One year his Christmas card showed him on the beach with an alligator the size of Jaws on a leash. Seriously. He's that kind of badass. He does this all behind dark shades. I don't know if I've ever seen his eyes.

I inch my hand out, not sure I want a rooster there. MD offers the mean-looking bird, who clucks and ruffles its feathers, then settles in my palm. And there it sits, beady eyes blinking away, head bouncing in anticipation of whatever the hell roosters anticipate. Bird in hand, I reach up to stroke it, and realize MD has vanished.

This pattern I recognize, his ability to come and go without notice, to step off the grid until he pops up a few years later with a few generalities as if he'd never been gone. He discards cell phones and changes telephone numbers. He doesn't bother with the Internet. No e-mail either. But once a year I'll receive a Christmas card, the recent ones invoking Christ's birth. I know nothing about one of my oldest friends beyond what I can see. About fifteen years back a woman collared him, dragging him across the country to California to grow fruit and nut trees and live off her real-estate investments. He tried to make a go with the trees, sending photographs of his orchards, standing proudly before an almond and apricot grove. When he finally left California and her, I didn't know for three years. He turned up at his cousin's house back in South Carolina.

What I see: A man who can just as easily show me how to operate a backhoe as how to steal gasoline from the company tank, open a beer bottle with a lighter, and appreciate good moonshine. A man who takes in stray alligators and kittens, nursing them the same. A man who drinks pints of Jim Beam "for the pain," and grows weed in the jungles of his backyard just because he can. A man who used to charm tourists daily with local stories that, when necessary, were dramatically enhanced to satisfy the tourist's need for a compelling tale to return home with and to minimize whatever work or favor the tourist was asking of him. A man who knows where to get the best sunset shot (over the marsh) and writes articles for *The Gamecock*, a hundred-year-old journal for the amateur and professional cocker. A man who is well versed in both the Bible and Hunter S. Thompson. A man who has moonlighted as a construction foreman, painter, landscaper, critter catcher, house sitter, earth mover, real-estate agent, and shrimp-boat crew. A man who distrusts the government and makes the majority of his income in cash. A man who smiles more often than he frowns. A man who will always be your friend first, while waiting for you to give him a reason not to be, which you probably will eventually. A man who hides behind dark glasses but gives you the feeling that he is opening his life to you, though he isn't, not at all.

I've never met or heard MD speak about anyone from his family, except for an adult daughter from an early marriage. I didn't really know where he was from until this visit, my first to the family farm. He's never spoken of a childhood, though he must have had one. I know almost nothing about his past other than snippets I've picked up over the years, some of which I don't trust. Or maybe I've filled in the gaps and don't trust what I've substituted. Some of those snippets involve a history in the boxing ring, which may just tell me more about MD's interest in cockfighting than anything else. I found a few articles online from the early eighties that told me my friend had indeed enjoyed a short and not so celebrated career as a heavyweight boxer. I found a photograph from a local newspaper that showed him sparring before he and another heavyweight featured in a match that night. Another article told me that MD lost his fight.

MD's career as a boxer (according to *BoxRec*):
won 2 (KO 2) + lost 3 (KO 3) + drawn 0 = 5 career professional bouts
Rounds boxed 8 KO% 40

If MD were a gamecock, he'd be dead.

In the photograph MD looks much the same, shock of curly hair, bushy mustache (I imagine he was born with the thing), tall and lean with railroad-tie arms that seem able to beat back anything that comes his way. I try to imagine him in the ring, but despite the powerful frame and cool demeanor I can't see him pounding an opponent. I can recall him removing the head of a rattlesnake with a swift blade and gutting a deer. But beating another man with his fists, even if those fists are gloved—

Still, it's also hard to conceive of my large friend losing any sort of fight. I've heard tale of later fights in the nineties, what would have been well past his prime. Rumors of an amateur caged fight and bear-wrestling. But why would he bother, a former professional boxer? For another stab at some tarnished glory, or was it simply for the amplified prize money? MD never turned down an opportunity to make an extra buck or two. And why have I never heard these stories before? Why does my friend guard his past so closely? I want to ask but some questions just don't come out easily. Or maybe I prefer the mythology to what is likely a less romantic version of the truth, like that career boxing record.

When MD returns he carries another bird. And orange rubber caps that look like thimbles.

"You put two of these birds in front of one another," he said, "and they'll fight until the other one is dead. That's all they know. Nothing unnatural about it."

Roosters fight not because they're mean, or bloodthirsty killers, but because they are born to protect and proliferate the species. They will sacrifice themselves to a predator to protect their brood. They will fight anything they perceive as a threat, from a human to a dog to another rooster.

He fits the orange rubber caps, called boxing gloves, over the roosters' natural spurs.

"So they don't kill each other."

In other places, MD tells me, where cockfighting is a significant and more accepted part of the culture, such as the Philippines, Indonesia, Puerto Rico, Mexico, and Thailand, fighters augment their birds with "blades" they fasten to the rooster's feet to ensure a bloodier fight. In North America, this practice of arming the birds is generally unpopular, he says, but he shows me some of the knives used in other countries. He shows me one the shape of a curved ice pick, its end sharpened to cut. I'm not sure why he has them.

"The birds will do the job without these blades. No need to give them weapons," he says, running his thumb over the razor-sharp blade until blood bubbles on his skin. "This one's Mexican."

Later I learn that so is his assistant, a middle-aged man who serves as MD's pitter, the one who handles the birds at a fight. All MD has to do is watch over the heads of the other gamblers like a prizefighter's promoter.

"I'm going to let them spar with the gloves on to show you how they fight. The gloves will keep them from goring each other. Of course, if we let them, they'll stomp on each other until one's dead. Doesn't matter if their spurs are covered or not. They won't stop. Roosters will trample, peck, and scratch each other to death. Whatever it takes." He watches the birds as they flap and burst at one another, striking like snakes.

"Why?" I ask, nervous that what he says might come true. But he is only being practical. Protecting his investment from unnecessary harm. This is commerce. Not art. Not a philosophical stance. And I'm pretty sure I don't want to watch a bird die.

MD holds the roosters, one in each hand. Already they've begun to peck at each other. But as soon as he drops them, they're at it before their feet hit the dirt. The great feathered coronas around their necks, called hackle, flare for a fight. The birds use their feet like some medieval iron claw. They stab with their beaks. They jump and fly, each aiming to top the other. Dust rises around them. They jab like a needle on a sewing machine. They aim their claws for the throat, the chest, and other meaty parts. When one finds flesh and draws blood, MD pulls them apart again and holds them on either side of his body. Just as quickly as the birds became enraged, they calm. Like most fights, it's over in seconds, but not before somebody gets bloodied. If you've ever been in a physical fight, no matter how short and spastic, which most are, you understand the rush of adrenaline that leaves you shaking afterwards. Almost embarrassed at how you've lost control and hurt somebody, been hurt, or both—but emboldened too. The only fights I've ever fought were chaos, fists windmilling, mouth open dumbly, eyes closed. No craft at all, just survival and surprise that such energy waits within.

"They're vicious, but not so bright. Like babies who forget you're there if they can't see you." MD grins beneath his bushy mustache.

My instance of witness is heightened as over a hundred birds crow their passion and swagger. Like inmates in a prison yard, they can smell a fight.

Confession: it was riveting watching these two beautiful animals go at each other, so intent on harming one another. I was both terrified and in awe. Not the first to be drawn by the primal. A fowl fight club. I saw no blood, no eyes dangling from sockets, no exposed white flesh. No dead birds. Just a few loose and ruffled feathers, some twitchy roosters, and a small dust cloud in the air at our knees. MD didn't let the fight last long—these were his birds and he had no intention of letting them get hurt. I'd enjoyed a surge of adrenaline and discovered something beautiful in the brief bout. Why was I drawn to the fighting cocks? Perhaps I envied them their purity, in the way they attacked. The birds reacted from instinct. There were no evil intentions, just an innate need to protect what is theirs. One will win and one will lose. There were no agonizing rituals of self-examination or ethics. They don't seek each other out, they don't attack out of malice, but defend as they were born to do. I enjoyed the simplicity of the fight for survival that governed their lives.

I needed a reason to find beauty, which I did, in the fight. For no such simplicity exists in my life. I'd seen the savagery of instinct in the birds themselves, but I'd also witnessed the savagery of intellect, man's need to manipulate the world, to cage and control the chaos. Or, as too often occurs, witnessed another news cycle that details a mass shooting in a mall, church, or elementary school. One man's desperate attempt to create order through what he can more easily destroy. While my life is generally governed by knowledge, experience, general intelligence, rules, ethics, and limited chance, these birds relied almost entirely on instinct and chance to guide them. But I'm the one who wears a night guard when I sleep/don't sleep to keep from grinding my teeth to nubs, leaving them rocking in my gums like trees in loose soil. I'm the one who needs three drinks each night, and whatever else it takes, to smooth out the ruffled feathers. I'm the one who tosses and turns in bed as I go over and over the lists in my head: of things to do and problems to solve. I'm the one who fears for my family's safety every time they leave the house without me, as if by somehow acknowledging and fretting over it, I can protect them from harm. I'm the one who paces my house as I gnaw on a fingernail, already gnawed to the quick, when things go awry, frantic to fix the problem immediately, to make it go away so that I can return to some sense of order, some sense that I'm in control. A lie I find comforting, if only temporarily.

"There will be blood because it's in their blood," MD says when he catches me brooding.

Did he really say that? I don't know, but I'm pretty sure. It sounds both like something he would and would never say.

His reply sounds like a rationalization to me. And I am prepared to walk away, to say I've seen enough. Twist open the bottle of Beam's Choice and work through some nostalgia, maybe smoke a joint. I am there to see my friend—the birds aren't a part of the deal. But now I'm thinking about them and my old friend and am I scrapping out survival and what the fuck am I doing every day? Is MD the bird? Am I? Does somebody have to be the bird? Am I fucking dying?

"We're no better. We tear each other apart every day. People spend their whole lives figuring out ways to hurt each other," he says.

MD returns the birds to their tiny plots of dirt and grass and blue barrel, and we leave to grab dinner and drinks.

We drive with the windows down as twilight descends, cold beers between our legs, the salty air at our faces. I want fried seafood, and the best is always found in places that call themselves shacks, so that's where we head. I feel far removed from the sidewalks of Atlanta, my tidy home, my day job behind a desk and before a classroom, my wife and daughter. I feel like I haven't lately—like I am adventuring again, like I can leave the day to chance, which I pretty much do since MD rarely tells me what comes next. I have only the clothes I've flown in, a cell phone, which I've turned off, and I don't care where I sleep, mostly. I'm not in the jungles of Chile or exploring the narrow alleys of Tangier, but it is far enough from the responsibilities of my daily life to feel foreign.

On paper my life has little romantic flair at all. I'm a writer but a quiet one. A public persona is not a requirement of my art, though it seems to be more and more necessary, something to which I futilely pander and alternately resist. I prefer off rather than on the grid, my privacy, my (former) lack of presence on the Internet, my hermit life. I spend a great deal of time at home and have no complaints. By day I teach and take care of my daughter, by night hang with my wife and daughter, read (aloud and not), and write, sometimes watch an episode of *Louie* on Netflix. I have lived and recalled more adventurous times of travel and life abroad, but lately, in a global culture with easy access to the rest of the world, travel and life abroad are rarely adventurous or without a clear and knowledgeable path. And like most fathers, the unexpected no longer has the same romantic appeal. It now means hospitals and illnesses, car accidents and bad weather, ruptured plumbing and infestations, odd pains and scary lumps, the late-night-jolt-you-from-sleep bumps and telephone calls: the commonplace but feared. The unexpected has a way changing your life entirely in seconds. You know this. And everything happens so fast, life and death, life and death just inches from each other. And you know this: that you will one day suffer in some way, large or small, and lose this fight.

Once you've hit middle age, seeing old friends after some time away can be an unsettling reminder that you too have aged, that you too have changed in ways you aren't aware of but everyone else can see, especially those who haven't seen you in a while. You don't get to see yourself age but through others. Getting old sucks and there is nothing like finding your reflection in your aging friends to remind you of this. But there's comfort there too. Over dinner we talk more about the birds and the fighting circuit.

"Take me with you to a fight," I say, feeling brave, feeling like those roosters in the yard. "I'll help."

"All right," MD says.

And there it is. He will show me what goes on at a real cockfight, and I can write about it. I want to do this. I need to get close to this primitive act. "In an objective way," I qualify.

"Just see what you see," he says.

I want to see what a real fight, without the gloves, looks like. I want to smell the birds and the people—those I imagine in cowboy boots, flannel shirts and mustaches, lots of mustaches. I want to hear the shouts of the cockteaser and the squawking, clucking of the cocks. I want to smell blood in the air and the earthy stink of dogs and hay, the whiff of a new cigarette, and taste the tinny bitterness of cold beer from a can. I want to spread hands dirty with mud and grass across my blue jeans, wipe a bandanna across my sweaty face in the heat and humidity of Lowcountry air. I want to feel the pulse of pure instinct, the surge of adrenaline that comes with a fight, the rubbery legs and shaking hands. Too much of my life is removed from the physical. I need to get my hands dirty.

From across the table, MD looks older. His knees are shot—from boxing or a lifetime of labor, I'm not sure. But it has left him hobbled and slightly bent. I don't remember him like this. His hair, still a curly shock, has grown out to his shoulders, a wiry, indistinct gray, like a weathered Parrothead with blown-out flip-flops and a fading tattoo. He's bent more at the shoulders. His mustache is still there, bushy but drooping and seeded with ash and that weird yellow color that usually comes with older smokers, though MD has never been one. There is Mark Twain in that mustache. Crow's feet cut rivers from his eyes, what I can see of them. He wears mirrored sunglasses until he switches to reading glasses for the menu. His skin is tanned and coarsened by days in the sun. His massive hands are scarred, scabbed, and calloused. I imagine him shucking oysters, the oyster knife slipping and slicing into his palm. Hands that have toiled and fought. He has lived close to the earth and under the sun.

There is a photograph of MD, another friend, and me during my one summer on the beach—two college boys framed by MD's massive arms. It's late somewhere and we are in full beach-bum attire—locals, not tourists. We are tanned, unshaven, bleached, and shaggy-haired. We are young, lean and muscled in cut-off t-shirts and blue jean shorts. Our faces are red with drink. MD holds up the bottle of Jim Beam that will eventually do us all in, leaving my college friend in the road out front, luckily for him rarely used. The self-timed photograph captures a moment of our friendship, but it also captures young men, at least two of whom know little about the world. The third, MD, stares back with the same calm, the same veiled eyes. MD seemed old to me then. But he was hardly thirty. Ten years later we would recreate that same photograph: the same stance, the same expressions, the same Jim Beam. Only ten years into our future and little had changed. It is only when I look at the most recent reenactment that I appreciate the time that has passed. We are mature men now: no longer lean but loose and thick with age. We all wear our age differently, one paunchier, another more wrinkled, one grayer. We all have our hair, most of it anyway—that's something, I suppose. I don't know if we are more ourselves now or less. Are we truer to our nature now than we were then? Isn't that what we all hope for in middle age, that we are the improved (not new) version of ourselves? That we should have found our truest selves by now? MD, a cockfighting, salt-of-the-earth, Lowcountry boy. Or, MD, a professional boxer, if a losing one, and a huckster. Me, a writer and a teacher who gets to read, write, and talk about books all day. Or, me, a lazier, fatter, safer version of the young man in the photograph.

My world is insular: my daughter's elementary school, work (another school), nearby friends, and a few regular restaurants and bars. Lots of weekend trips and local events to look forward to, but with a nine-year-old in tow, absent the ability to pursue anything with too much of the unknown. When you're with a child you don't want things to unravel. With more at stake in my life now, and out of fear of what might and can certainly turn wrong, I insist on constant governance. Only when I'm alone, i.e., without my family, can I let life unfold as it will, no matter how much I try to contain it. I recall adventures of my twenties and thirties and marvel at the person I was then. Reckless, curiosity unbound, with the will to pursue my imagination wherever it led. Now I rely on rules, guidelines, and an understanding of my environment—the known versus the unknown—to ensure nothing foul happens to my family or me, that every undertaking goes well. There is just as much superstition involved as there is actual control. If I don't anticipate what might happen, it will. I don't gamble. Sure, some of my caution is that of a father and a husband, unease for a family on whom I keep a watchful eye. I don't surrender and I don't fear death, in whatever form it may take. My apprehension grows from my desire to live longer, to see my daughter grow up, to be her father for as long as possible. I'm not scared to die, I just don't want to. I know the consequences are that I probably don't allow enough mystery and spontaneity in my daughter's life. That seems as tragic as other kinds of loss. But to believe that we are ever truly at the helm in this life is naïve and foolish, chasing the tail of some windswept fantasy of control. Nature bats us around like a balloon at a kid's birthday party. How do we reconcile that? And what kind of shadow have I become?

Visiting MD I feel of the world again, not pressed to the bed for fear of what moves outside. I feel like MD's roosters, my feathers ruffled, back to fighting strength, on the offensive, ready to take the helm and not lie down just yet, driven by a purely physical need to be in the world.

When we come back from dinner, MD pulls himself out of his rental car, no easy task for a man so large in a car so small. He rented the car for my visit. I have no idea how he gets around otherwise. He hobble-hustles over to the fence gate.

"Uh oh," he says, pulling open the gate.

"What?"

"Dogs got in the yard." He points to something I can't see. "Not good."

And sure enough, a lamb lies on its side, blood smeared across the white fleece of its throat.

"Baby, just three weeks old."

MD walks off without another word, searching the large yard. His gait is deliberate but sluggish. I stare at the animal. I don't flinch. Blood stains its body but there are no other signs of violence. The lamb looks to be napping. The image holds me. This is no road kill, no photograph. I feel as if I stand upon an alien landscape. Just like that I am transported from the routine of my life to this extraordinary moment. The fleece where there is no blood looks soft and bleached. I want this moment, this life and now death. As if the lamb's death brings me close enough that I don't have to witness anything closer. I want to touch the lamb's wool but when I bend my knees and reach for the softness of its fleece flies burst into buzzing around my hand. MD comes back carrying two more lambs by their hind legs. He tosses them beside the one that still holds my gaze.

"Dogs got 'em. Nothing but instinct, doing what dogs do. Probably shook 'em by the neck like a stuffed toy. They were just playing," MD says as he stands over the three dead lambs. "Don't know any better."

These deaths are routine, something that goes on every day. This is the reality. That any moment nature can take over and change your life. I'm not crazy, I'm not a paranoid depressive. This is real. The first time I witnessed the crossing of this line was when my father died of lung cancer in the span of six very short months, not because he smoked, which he did, but simply because his cells mutated and turned bad. Animals kill other animals, both the pattern and chaos of nature, of which we are a part. Too often we separate ourselves from the other animals, the other parts of nature, the universe. How do we deserve such separation? Only in our ability to think it do we distinguish ourselves. Yet chaos still reigns, no more and no less because we fear it, because we know it will one day happen. We can no more control dogs outside a fence than we can the guy who drops his phone as he speeds through a red light, T-boning your wife and daughter as they drive for ice cream on a warm Saturday night. No more than the sad and alienated gunman who turns up in your shopping mall to spray the crowd with exploding bullets from an assault rifle. The flash flood that sweeps your car from the road, trapping you and your family inside as water fills the cabin. The bullet returning to earth after celebratory gunfire that travels from one neighborhood to another and into your yard on New Year's Eve and lodges in the brain of your four-year-old who only wanted to stay up until midnight and light sparklers before she went to bed. The accidental poisoning of your best friend when he buys tainted ground beef at the grocery store. The blood vessel that bursts in your head as you wrap a towel over your daughter's shoulders and lift her out of the bath.

So, as nature demands, we fight back, we keep our talons up and our coronas flared, not to die, but to live. I'm sure I think of a way I or someone I love might cross that line every day. Most concern car accidents and cancer, big killers for sure. But there is no shortage of ways to die, more than the imagination can conceive, always some shadow waiting to consume us. Children leave you like this—legless against the fear of losing them. Even fear of your own death is driven by a desire not to leave your child parentless. Being here again near the water with the old friend I still know little about reminds me to live a little closer to the line. Just as MD keeps himself in the ring.

The flock of sheep rests in the shade of a sprawling live oak. They chew at grass, nibble at fleas, and swish their tails at flies. There is no sense that violence has occurred here today. A ewe stares at me without blinking. In the last twenty-four hours, three of her lambs have been killed. Is she aware of this? Is there an intimation of the loss or even of the mortality that surrounds her? Or has she already forgotten, her memory of birth and life and death only as far as she can see and smell, only as real as the living things before her, the dead things by the fence no longer in her care?

We settle into the beers.

"That's shitty about the lambs," I say. I want him to help me make more of what I've seen, what I've photographed and already Instagrammed to embellish what doesn't need embellishment, to make the death of three lambs count.

"Yeah, weakness in the fence somewhere. My fault," he says. "Doesn't matter—they'll get in one way or another."

Is this true? Dogs get in fences one way or another? If so, why have lambs if they are just to be gotten by blood thirsty, playful dogs? Dogs who are supposed to be guarding the fence. And who's watching my fence, I wonder? Are they the same ones who will also find a way in and rob you of those you love? Our best bet is to bob and weave at whatever is thrown at us, never stop moving, never let your guard down. And understand that, even with a vigilant defense, the punches will get through. I feel as if this breach in the fence is my fault, as if my fear of the unknown and random led to this. Of course it's not true but I want MD to know I'm sorry. "I'm sorry," I say.

"It's nothing," he says and pulls himself out of his La-Z-Boy like a giraffe, legs unbuckling and pushing his heft upwards. "Another day."

I leave the next morning, vowing to come back in the fall when it's cooler, to follow MD on the cockfighting circuit through a few stops in the Southeast. We shake and nod, neither of us really believing I'll be back. And, sure enough, as I settle into my airplane seat and prepare for the short flight home, I know that I won't. I've seen enough of the line between life and death for a while. Still, every now and then I need to be reminded that it's there, to remember what's worth protecting on this side.

MD is a good man. Evidence here might suggest another kind: callous, violent, and uncultured. But that is not my friend at all. Like the roosters he raises and fights, he is a creature of survival: bob and weave in the ring, duck and cover, kick up dirt for his life. A few months later I try to call him but the last number he gave me has been disconnected. Most of us live as if we don't know we're going to die. I will never see that cockfight. Though maybe the idea of the cockfight is enough. My fight is here.

Out of Place

Nicole Walker

Birds of prey weren't new to me. Driving through southern Utah, I'd seen them from the car, sitting on fence posts that had been put up to keep the cattle from wandering onto I-15 and that now provided perches for Red-tailed Hawks. On the way home from Capital Reef one winter, I saw five Bald Eagles, standing as tall as fence posts by the side of the road. On the ground, they were undignified, tearing at a roadkilled deer. But when, in my review mirror, the head of one eagle turned nearly all the way around to make sure I was on my way, its white head eclipsing the thin, exhaust-dirty snow, the eagle made it clear that I had interrupted them. On the side of the road tugging meat was where the eagles were supposed to be. I was the one out of place.

I wonder if this is how the world ends, climate change revealing origins, transplants, hybrids. The end-of-the-world spoiler: we are not as original as we thought we were.

Compared to southern Utah, western Michigan seemed like the last place you'd see birds of prey. Once, my husband Erik, my daughter Zoë, and I tried to go camping. We drove and drove until we found a campground far from the city. As we unpacked the car and began to set up the tent, I saw a basketball hoop. The campground was next to a neighborhood.

No matter how hard I tried, I couldn't make Grand Rapids feel like home. Grand Rapids was not Salt Lake, where I had lived for most of my life. I'd left for college, stayed in Portland for a few years, went back to Salt Lake for grad school. Now in Grand Rapids, having moved for a job, I wanted to go home. In time I would get used to this place, I knew, in the same way one gets used to oneself: You learn to like the way your hair parts on the left, the way your left eye is smaller than your right, the way you bite your pinky fingernail just like your mother. You learn to adapt to the place you live. But as the climate changes, as even your native land changes—butterflies in November!—I wonder how you're supposed to get used to that.

But I also felt as though I should stay away from Salt Lake. That place has a way of domesticating even the most wild child, and Zoë, my three-year-old, though stubborn with her love of square food and her rabbit-like dialect, wasn't particularly wild. She liked her face and her hands clean, her hair brushed. She folded cloth napkins straight from the dryer. She suggested that we get out the iron before company comes, like my mom did. I wanted her, even if it was a pain in my ass, to be *more* stubborn, less acquiescent. Fierce. If we went back to Salt Lake, I was afraid my daughter would follow my path—would fall for boys who said they liked the way she laughed at their unfunny jokes, the way she asked which direction to turn, right or left, although she knew full well already, the way she put her pinky finger in her mouth. Just like I do. Just like my mom does.

Grand Rapids, April 5th. And this was the first time Zoë and I, except for one freakishly warm week in January, had seen the sun. There was only residual snow on the ground. We could finally see grass. We looked for early flowers over at Aquinas College across the street from our house. The college's budget was hemorrhaging but the hemorrhage had become beautiful. The unfunding let these typically manicured lawns and flower beds turn back to wild.

On the campus, we found purple-striped crocuses. Zoë wanted to collect all this newness. She said, let's pick the flowers. I told her, no, the flower lasts longer in the ground than in your hand. Not much longer, but longer. I distracted her with a stick that had fallen from a sycamore tree and the promise, as I pointed to a little boy's Big Wheel, that we would get her a Big Wheel. Keep her moving, I thought.

The little boy's dad, who saw us pointing at the Big Wheel, asked if we had seen the owls. What owls? I asked. I had been satisfied by crocuses and the promise of daffodils, but now I was excited.

"Come on," the dad said. "I'll show you." We walked across the Catholic college campus, past the Jesus sculpture, toward the middle of a tiny parking lot. The kids followed us—his on the Big Wheel, mine mastering the art of curb-walking.

"Look at the No Parking sign, then look straight up," the dad said.

In the branches of a giant sycamore, still dry with winter and naked against the first-time-in-six-months-blue-sky, sat two gigantic owls. They looked like Snowy Owls—so big and white and soft, the size of a big cat, maybe even a raccoon. But they were just chicks. Owlets. Babies.

"Look at the daffodils, already blooming. Usually owlets aren't born so early. They shouldn't even be hatching yet. These ones are premature."

I believed him. He had probably lived in the Midwest his whole life. He knew where flowers and wild animals collided. He even knew what type of owls they were—Barred, he said. He was half frontiersman, half gardener. Barred Owls try to get a jump on other species and lay their eggs in late March or early April, he told me. It was early April just now, and not only had the eggs already hatched, but these birds were halfway ready for flight.

The winter had been hard. But that one week in January had confused fertility hormones, leading animals to believe it was spring when it was still deep winter. Instead of waiting for March, the parent owls must have mated in January. These snow-colored owls were not the breed that usually matches snow-colored ground, and without that weird weather, I would not have been looking at those owls. It was only through the freak change of climate that I could see them.

Like all people who hate change, I read a lot of studies about global warming. When Zoë had been born seven weeks premature, leading to a chronic cough and a battery of MRIs, I looked for anything that would explain what had gone wrong. *The American Journal of Epidemiology* published an article titled "High Ambient Temperature and the Risk of Preterm Delivery" correlating climate change in California with preterm birth.

> A significant positive association was found between apparent temperature and preterm delivery during the warm season in California. Mean, maximum, and minimum apparent temperatures all had significantly elevated associations for lag days up to 1 week. When we considered vulnerable subgroups, all studied showed increased risks regardless of maternal age, racial/ethnic group, level of educational attainment, or infant's sex (1111).

The authors also commented on other studies indicating that environmental factors such as air pollution and high ozone levels contribute to preterm birth. Still other studies have shown that the smaller environment, that of the mother's body, contributes to preterm birth when it becomes infected by bacteria or suffers from high stress. There are many factors available for anyone who wants to try to explain the growing trend of premature babies. But it didn't matter which factor I considered—global or personal—neither made her cough go away.

Climate change seemed the most likely indicator for the owls' prematurity, but maybe the cause was something else. Nesting on a college campus, even a Catholic one, does weird things to hormones. Whatever the cause of their prematurity, these naked-in-trees owls, born not just early but out of season, would have a hard time of it at least for a while—if they even made it through spring.

The owls, big as preemie babies, stared back with wild eyes. The smaller one nudged its big sibling's wing, as though it wanted under, as though it wanted its mother. They looked caught, trapped somewhere they didn't want to be. Normally, they'd have unfurling leaves to hide behind. Shadows of bigger trees should, in May, conceal their furry heads, making them look not so big, not so obvious. In early April, their white down matched the color of the naked sycamores. But white is never camouflage against early spring sky. One owl stretched its tail out, full-fan nervous. I wanted to stop looking at them. I was making them nervous. We were all making them nervous. But how do you stop looking at something you've never seen before, even if you know they shouldn't be seen?

"The mother must be off hunting," the man said.

I looked around for her but it was hard to see with the sun in my eyes. Zoë, complaining about the sky being too bright, only looked up at the owls for a second. I thought she saw them. She blinked a few times in their general direction. She liked birds as much as I do, although she took them in stride. Like the crocuses, she thought she'd see another one around the corner.

"Leave them there," she said, mimicking what I'd said about flowers. "They'll live longer if you don't pick them."

We left the owl-man and his son and headed toward home. I hated leaving the owls. They looked hungry. But I had my own kid to feed. The sun, still crooked so early in spring, reminded me it was time to start making dinner. Zoë looks like me only in a certain light, but when she headed right for the kitchen, announcing she was hungry, her heredity was confirmed. Any enthusiasm or excitements led her, just as it did me, to the refrigerator. When something good happens to me, I want to commemorate the occasion with some fancy cheese or a thin slice of prosciutto. When she asked, "Can I have some blueberries or something?" the word "something" inflected upward. My voice, when I'm unsure about what it is I really want, ticks up too. I did what I could to find something that tasted like summer berries. I settled on "something" like grapes, which you can get all year long. I wondered what the owls would eat, born out of season. Could they substitute mouse for squirrel? Maybe the owls could get by on discarded dorm food and parking-lot French fries.

I laid the chicken breasts between wax paper and got out the rolling pin.

"Where's the pizza?" Zoë asked. She was used to rolling out pizza dough with me.

I showed her the chicken breast and point out how fat and uneven they are. "We've got to pound the breasts thin," I told her. "For chicken parmesan, they need to be half an inch thick. Do you want to try?"

She said yes, but she hit the breasts with no force at all.

"You have to hit them hard." I took the rolling pin from her and give the breasts a whack. They submitted, flattening out, becoming more dough than flesh.

In the middle of the next swing of the rolling pin, Zoë yelled for me to stop. "That hurts the chicken."

I understood her point. It was an odd thing to do: take these round breasts and make them flat. Chickens are factory-farmed to make their breasts so fat and thick that they topple forward with the weight, their beaks nailing the ground. It's ridiculous, I thought as I continued to pound their yellow flesh into smooth medallions, that the chicken growers spent so much time, energy, and DNA manipulation making their chickens grow their breasts unnaturally fat, and here I am, just thinning them out again. But that's the only way I knew how to make chicken parmesan.

We, cooks and raisers of chickens and children, think we can control the way things turn out, but how much control do we really have? Even geneticists lack the faith they once had. They used to believe that the only code was the DNA code; replicate, rinse, and repeat, and one could make a cell of a hamster into a baby hamster—with a little splicing and some warm sperm and the kind real estate of a surrogate womb. You could grow baby hamsters in the uterus of a rabbit. DNA predicted and predicated. Dolly the sheep was born as a one hundred percent replica of her mother. Except her mother lived a long life. Dolly lived briefly. She was sickly. Though identical to her mother, she was not the lamb her mother had promised her to be.

Chickens are both adapted and adaptable. Back and forth, the chickens adapted, then we adapted them, then they adapted to that adaptation and here I was, adapting them back. Adapting to a new situation is one thing. The owls, they adapted to a new climate, or at least they had survived from hatchlings to downy feathered branch-sitters. But adapting the situation to suit your chicken-parmesan needs—that is another kind of adaptation entirely.

Since I had forgotten to buy mozzarella for the chicken parmesan, I tore up string cheese and layered the strings across the chicken breasts that I'd "oven-fried" at four hundred degrees and topped with Prego. The string cheese, arcing under the heat, melted more like plastic than cheese. I hoped dinner wouldn't end up tasting like cheap burnt polyester. Adapting a recipe to suit your unwillingness to go to the store doesn't always turn out for the best.

The following morning, I went over to check on the owls. I told Erik I was going running since it would sound weird to say I was going to stare at tree branches with the hope that I'd see birds that weren't supposed to be there. I was sick to my stomach thinking they would be gone, that their mom has been driven off by the smoking college students and their loud cars, that someone has seen the babies and knocked them down, wanting to take them home as pets, that they were born too soon and the mother wasn't ready to feed them and they were starving up there in the tree and I wouldn't be able to tell because the downy fur made them look so soft and fat but even if I could tell, I didn't know how to grind up raw squirrel with my teeth and regurgitate into their mouths.

When I got to the sycamore trees, I couldn't see them at first. But then, suddenly, there they were—their little white bodies, two halves of one moon, and I was happy for a second until I thought of all the falling down that could happen. If I could have seen the mother for just one minute, I would have faith that these little chicks would not break my heart. But there was no mama bird swooping in with half-digested vole in her gullet and I was unsure about the role of mother birds here.

I'm unsure about the role of mothers anywhere. I wanted Zoë to be fierce but I also wanted her to be polite. I wanted her to be strong and yet forgiving. I wanted her to have all the friends and a best friend, to be the smartest in the class but not too aware of being the smartest, to feel free and yet rooted. I wanted oxymoron after oxymoron, just like my mom had. My mom wanted her daughters to know proper etiquette—we knew which fork to use when—coupled with feminism that insisted we take what was ours and not be demure. To this day, my sisters and I can eat more ounces of prime rib than any guy we've known.

Later, though, when my mom and I were talking about Joe, the fifteen-year-old boy I'd had sex with when I was twelve, and how I couldn't find the right word for too-early sex and she was telling me she was sorry, that it was her fault, that she shouldn't have let me hang out at a house where the parents weren't home, she explained why she did let me go over there so often.

She didn't want Joe's mom to think my mom didn't approve of her working. She did approve. She herself wanted to work outside of the house. She should have known better, she said. Insides of houses were the places where real danger happened.

"I should have known, what with what happened with me and my sisters and Uncle Dick, that men take girls into the bathroom and use them like tissues," she said.

"You can't generalize. Not all men do," I said.

She scoffed. "In our family, it's genetic." Then, instead of going on about our family history of inappropriate male behavior, she changed the subject. "I think Zoë needs some new shoes."

I didn't tell my mom how often I let her go barefoot in her own backyard. As a mother, she would have been OK with it. As a grandmother, she'd think it was too uncivilized. But I believed, as she had once, that you have to be a little wild sometimes in order to find out what you really are, even if it looks uncouth.

In the April 2007 issue of *The Economist,* the author of an epigenetics column reported on a study about free-range versus caged chickens. Free-range chickens born to mothers raised in cages behave, even outside the cage, like their mothers. Cages appear to physically alter the brain cells of domesticated chickens, which alter a chemical in the ovaries of the hens, sealing the fate of those free-range chicks. They cluck around as though they're in cages anyway, scooting to corners when they're nervous, waiting for someone to feed them rather than pecking the ground for seeds.

Imagine your future mapped chemically and genetically even before you were conceived. Things must be alterable. You pray there is something that will counteract whatever stress your mother may have experienced when young and trapped and domesticated by the overly familiar touch of an uncle or your best friend's brother. You don't want to "adapt" in this case. In this case, you want the situation to change. Adapt the world.

I lie on the bed with Zoë, who is asleep, and smell her hair and think, it's because I'm her mom that I can do this. I can stroke her arm. I can kiss her neck. There is a reason I can do this, I justify. I'm her mom. But that thought makes me dissociate. I hover above and see myself kissing her and it looks weird: too intimate. I scoot over, move away. Is this moving away the beginning of the gap? Does my own nervousness make space enough for someone else to move in and make her body familiar? Her familiar body was mine, cultivated by me. But someone else will find it wild and want to make it theirs. I would have done anything if it could make her stay three years old and under the crook of my arm forever, but my arm would cramp and her head would itch and we'd both start talking about our favorite foods and get hungry and have to get up. Our bodies usually win these arguments.

Between this wild rolling and that future, someone will move in to fill that gap, which, I guess, at some point, is natural too. I hope not a boy, not too soon. But I hope against history. I fear I've infected her already with this need to have somebody close to me. What if it was in my breast milk? What if it was my DNA?

But even now, already, when she kisses me, she holds me behind the neck and practically dips me, then kisses me fat on the lips. Even though she is only three years old, I see the sex approaching her. I recoil and recoil and then recover by talking to her. When she talks to me she is herself, not just body. When she talks, she signifies her immediacy, not her what-might-be.

Awake she is the funny baby who says, "I need to talk with you" and motions me over to hear the big news about what she's making me for dinner. "I'm making you some oats." She then pinches her fingers together and hands me a single oat. She sings, "I love Mom and Dad and the couch and the chair," and I think if she'll talk and sing always no one will put her in that place where her mother was put, and her grandmother before that: where the guy keeps telling her to be quiet and for some dumbass reason, she agrees.

Strands of ghost DNA follow our DNA like tracers. No geneticist could map it but it is as predictable as blond hair and blue eyes. This future is not predictable but it is traceable in hindsight: the *tsk tsk* my mother makes that I also make after someone suggests a heresy like putting ketchup on their scrambled eggs or spritzer in their wine. Identical eye rolls, my mom and I. If you could stop the DNA in its place and take an echo of those strands, you would see the T clutching the C and the A commingling with the G but you might also see the future: an aunt who won't look her uncle in the eye, a mother who glares at that same uncle at every family reunion, a different aunt pregnant and married at sixteen to the janitor who worked at the elementary school across the street, bile in the back of your throat after having gotten drunk the night before, not because you like beer but because it distracts you from what the guy who gave you the beer's hands are doing, a neighborhood boy telling you you're pretty, well, pretty enough to lead you down to the unfinished basement where a mattress lays like it was expecting you, a friend who watches, a dare to go out to a car with a boy you didn't know and just "see" what happens. I can hear the echoes in my body echoing in hers. I close my ears.

How to spare Zoë? Cluck around like a real wild chicken, Z. Not a free-range bird borne of a caged hen, I should tell her. Or maybe I should stop calling her chicken and call her some wild bird instead. I should make wild noises. Adapt her world. Keep her moving. Keep her away from native ground.

Could the owls, living in what might have once been their native space but is now space claimed by the city, hear what they needed to hear? I worried, late at night, that the owlets couldn't hear the sound of crickets, the chirping of frogs over I-96 as it sped along. Fulton Street, a main artery that runs into downtown Grand Rapids, bordered the college. In the way bats use echolocation to find their food or their way back home, owls use auditory space maps to hone in on their prey, to find their way back to their nests. How would the owlets learn to use that map if they couldn't hear their mother over the cars as she folded her quiet self around the noise of a mouse?

When I was pregnant, my food echoed in my body. I was gassy and bloated. I could feel right below my abdomen the round of the apple I'd just eaten. I could almost see the nest of spaghetti underneath my skin, just to the right of my uterus. And the food echoed in the baby. Every bite of red-leaf lettuce, full of folic acid, was ammunition against spina bifida. Every glass of milk grew a bit of femur, a centimeter of ulna.

Every meal is special when you're pregnant. You're all nurture now. Nature has done all she can with the making of the zygote, and your job now is to support that work—to not screw it up by neglecting your folic acid or calcium intake. Everyone watches what you eat, what you drink. If I had a French fry, I'd worry—what is this building in the baby? If I drank too much carrot juice, I wondered if the beta-carotene turned the baby, however briefly, orange.

Unlike eating, breastfeeding balances nature and nurture. The milk flows; it matters that you ate breakfast but not so much exactly what.

As the baby sucks, you stroke the side of her head. You watch with awe the fingers as they press on the side of the breast instinctively. You see how the dimple in her cheek matches the one in yours. Supposedly, breastfed babies learn to know when they're hungry and when they're full. Even if I ended up giving Zoë some mediocre DNA and inherited molestation baggage, I hope by breastfeeding I gave her a sense of food as nutrition and food as love, without one ever having to trump the other.

I think teaching Zoë to cook nurtures her more than feeding her does. I try to get her to eat nine different colors of vegetables and fruits a day, but when we're cooking, things aren't as serious. If she pokes a hole in the pizza dough, we press the dough back together. If she adds a little too much salt, we add a little more water. If she adds too much cream, it probably just tastes better anyway. Cooking requires some precision and control, but it's mostly a forgiving sport—there are always ways to mitigate mistakes.

I take great heart in just the title of Ethan Watters' essay "DNA Is Not Destiny." The article describes studies done on agouti mice. These mice are fat and yellow. Their parents were fat and yellow. It seems likely their children will be fat and yellow. These fat mice are susceptible to cancer and diabetes, as were their parents, as will be their children. Two scientists Jirtle and Waterland designed a genetic experiment around these mice. They produced mice that looked nothing like their parents. These mice were thin and brown. Regular mice. Did they splice the gene, fix the broken DNA? No, they changed the mother's diet just before she conceived the would-be fat rat. So while she still handed down those same old lousy genes, the genes read differently.

> Starting before conception, Jirtle and Waterland fed a test group of mother mice a diet rich in methyl donors, small chemical clusters that can attach to a gene and turn it off. These molecules are common in the environment and are found in many foods, including

> onions, garlic, and beets and in the food supplements often given to pregnant women. After being consumed by the mothers, the methyl donors worked their way into the developing embryos' chromosomes and onto the critical agouti gene. The mothers passed along the agouti gene to their children intact, but thanks to their methyl-rich pregnancy diet, they had added to the gene a chemical switch that dimmed the gene's deleterious effects (*The Best American Science and Nature Writing 2007* 277).

By changing the mama rat's diet, the scientists changed the mouse's body response to this gene. The call and response that usually goes fat and yellow echoed back brown and thin. Epigeneticists argue against the idea that genes are fate. They see applications for cancer, rheumatoid arthritis, neurodegenerative diseases like Alzheimer's and diabetes.

Environment can change things. Food is one's primary environment. "Life-long 'methylation diets' may be the trick to staying healthy," Watters writes. Genes aren't deaf. They listen to the surrounding sound. This is good news, I think, for the agouti mice and for me and for Z. The problem to solve becomes less about how we cannot control our DNA or our inherited baggage but how we can control our environment. We can change, or at least influence the DNA. Zoë loves onions. She'll eat a whole Walla Walla sweet onion like an apple. Imbibe those methylenes, little Z, I tell her. Defend against your mom's predilections and habits, her distractions and substitutions, her thick waist and her short legs. I think back. I ate a lot of onions before I got pregnant. Countries of them. When I was pregnant, my friend Matt made a four-onion soup and I didn't let a single *Allium cepa* escape.

I went one more time to check. I couldn't find the owls anywhere. Their attempt to make a wild place in the city had failed. The owls had either died or found a real wild. Should I hope that they'd learned to adapt? That this city environment could work for them—that students, in throwing out burned French fries, half-eaten sandwiches, healthy snacks from home, could bring squirrels? Every square foot, you saw a squirrel. Maybe this was the exact right place for two Barred owls. Positive thoughts, I told myself. I looked further.

The canopy of trees never appeared as big as when I scanned them for something small. I looked through the branches into the sky breaking through.

I looked down for any still, dead white bodies. When I looked up again, I saw flashes of white everywhere—owls on every branch. I looked straight ahead. Don't look up again. I let myself believe that the trees were full of owls. Owls. They live here. There are plenty of squirrels. Maybe even owls can adapt the world to them, can make their own Edens.

Zoë won't eat the chicken. She says, "It's not square." As I jump up to cut the chicken into the square shape she likes for fear she will decide to eat nothing at all—something a born-too-early preemie can't afford to do—I can see who has adapted to whom.

She still won't eat it. I try to reframe the issue for her. "The owls would eat it."

I can tell immediately I've said the wrong thing. I've reminded her of the owls, of the bird-like nature of chickens. She pokes at her mozzarella. It's stringy as plastic. I go to the fridge to get her something, anything, to eat.

But she's not a preemie anymore. And sometimes you have to learn to adapt to what you've got. The owls, still surviving too early in the spring in their downtown habitat, are doing it.

I sit back down in my chair, take a bite of my chicken.

I look up at her. She takes a bite of her mozzarella. She is at home in her body, eating what she likes, eating what I like, eating what I don't like. She holds her ground. I get up, tear her another bite of chicken. She takes another bite of plastic cheese, putting me in my place. I look at her and the camera agitates. You don't have to move often or a lot, I think. The world shakes of its own accord, makes space between history and future, between strands of DNA. She is me and she is not me. In the gap between her chair and mine, she does not fall. In the space between she and me, I see displays of branch, the shimmer of light, the forest that, even in the middle of a city, still finds a way to feed a couple of baby owls, born too early. Zoë, her eyes wild and fierce, chewing plastic mozzarella, defying her mother's desire for her to eat chicken, but conceding, as her mother does, to eat a bit of the cheese, going further than her mother and even trying a taste of the Prego, adapts to her own shaky native ground.

Reflections of a Moderately Disturbed Grandfather

Joe Mackall

As the day nears dusk, I watch as my oldest granddaughter runs out of our house toward a car full of other high school kids. The girl behind the wheel—somewhere between sixteen and the rest of her life—is a little overweight, which for some reason comforts me, until I notice she wears the too-thick makeup of a young woman wanting a life she doesn't yet understand. A boy jumps out of the rustbelt Buick to let Ellie in the backseat. I don't like the kid right off; I know he can't be trusted. His movements are too deliberate. He acts as if perpetually aware of a camera. He has too-beautiful hair. He doesn't even acknowledge my wife or me as we smile miserably from the front porch. I hear the tinkling of an empty can spilling out of the car and hitting our driveway. Assuming it's a Miller or Bud, I tense; my muscles clench. I then feel the warmth of my wife's fingers on my arm, which is just enough to keep me still. Ellie tosses us a casual wave over her shoulder and disappears into the Buick, into the world. The world outside of our family and our home has been whispering to her since she was old enough to realize there was something else out there. It beckons us all, of course. But on this day, it echoes with the wail of pain.

But I'm just imagining this. Ellie's only four years old. She still has her favorite blanket she calls her "night night." She never runs out of our house unless it's to play in our yard. As a matter of fact, she hates leaving our home, even to go back to her own, to parents she loves and who love her. But I know this will change. It has to. It's the way of the world, which is little consolation. I recall being eager for my own three children to grow up, accrue resources for living, become independent. When it comes to my granddaughters, however, I'm often paralyzed with fear at the thought of their entering the wider world. And I'm not exactly sure why.

I admit I've been blindsided by becoming a grandfather. Before we had grandkids, I'd professed my vision of our life to come. I told my wife, Dandi, that we'd buy the kids anything they needed, take them on vacations, pay for college, leave them money, make sure they had the best life and most boundless love we could give them, but I did not want to be involved in the day to day. I did not see myself as a babysitter or as a second layer of parent. I did not want my life defined by becoming a grandfather. My desire was to drift in the sweet stratosphere of benign neglect. Dandi has promised to waterboard me if I ever express a desire to walk around a mall wearing a "World's Greatest Grandpa" T-shirt.

Now I can't go more than three or four days without aching to see the girls. My whole way of being wavers in their presence. My dark disposition begins to lighten up; at least it does when they're around. I figured out some of it. After a quarter century of loving all the same people, I've fallen in love with somebody new. I've loved my children all of their lives and my wife every day for nearly twenty-five years, but now there's new love. Perhaps my heart's tectonic shifts have shaken my psychic geography. I have two new people to love, two new people to see the world through, to share life with, to worry about, to fear for in a time when I sometimes can't recognize my own country and when the world's people appear easily connected electronically and so dangerously disconnected in just about every other conceivable way.

I often feel as though I'm moving toward the edge of a foreign land, the plains of an emotional dystopia. I know it's connected in ways I don't fully understand to life as a grandfather and as a man in his fifties, life as an American in a country increasingly polarized, fracked, outsourced, downsized, and droned, teetering on the dream-edge of itself. As a writer, editor, a full tenured professor, I have work I love and am still young and coherent enough to do. I also know what's out there waiting for me: impotence, probably; incontinence, likely; dementia, some adverb I can't come up with right now; senior moments, surely, and then, surely, no moments at all. I have a great family, a wife I cherish, loving children, and two wondrous granddaughters. My father's alive and well and lives (for the warm months of the year) a couple miles from me. My granddaughters too live only minutes away. My son is healthy and happy and married to a young woman I adore. And just beyond all this peace and love I perceive the vague existence of foreboding or surrender or something I've not allowed myself to imagine. I'm gazing through paradise and seeing into the shadow of the fall.

My oldest granddaughter, Ellie, lives awash in awe and wonder, and she's even splashed some of it onto my penchant for lazy cynicism and dark moods. When it rains, she wants to run outside and hold it as it falls. "Let's go catch the rain, Pa." That's who I am to her: Pa. "The stars are like candles in the sky, Pa." When my daughter asked what I'd like the kids to call me, I was ready with a name: Santiago. Granted it would have been tough for a toddler to say, but I figured one could learn in time. It beat the hell out of being called "bappo" or "fafa" or "gragra" or some other hideous title. I gave up on Santiago, however, when I imagined the girls referring to me as "Sans" until they could say Santiago. It would be as though my name to them were "without." As in sans serif. I just couldn't live with being without. I like the sound of Pa; it's solid, permanent. Pa's what the boy called his dad The Rifleman on the eponymous show. And also how Ben's *Bonanza* boys addressed him. Pa sounds like the frontier; it pushes through the small universe of our home with the gravitas of time and history, even if only pop-culture history.

I used to love July 2 for literary reasons, and I would take the day off no matter where I was employed, volunteering to work on the fourth for anybody who wanted to trade with me. I honored this day because both Chekhov and Hemingway died on July 2, albeit nearly sixty years apart. Now it's my holiday because on July 2, a month before she turned two, Ellie said, as casual as you please when I walked into the room, "Hi, Pa," for the first time.

I also revere the day Ellie learned to say the word *No*. I laugh the celebratory laugh of the mad whenever Ellie says it. "No, Pa. No, Momma. No bath. No, Dadda. No home. No carrots. No. No. No." And the louder and more aggressively she says it, the louder I laugh and the more I celebrate. All young girls ought to scream the word No—early and often.

Every time Ellie's over she rings a small bell by our open kitchen window to summon birds to their feeder. And sometimes, as if she's been transformed into a diminutive disciple of St. Francis, they fly to her. I so succumb to her view of the world at moments like this that it's hard for me to imagine that not every bird on every tree in a thousand-mile radius doesn't hasten to the sound of this child's bell. This is part of what frightens me. She has weakened my foundation. If I'm cynical and skeptical and given to dark moods and the unforgiving but familiar company of the black dog, I'm psychically safe—at least, that's the myth I've lived by. Don't leave yourself too vulnerable to things like hope and optimism and faith. Like Robert Duvall's character in the film *Tender Mercies*, "I don't trust happiness. Never did." Perhaps Ellie's wonder is nothing more than the lingua franca of innocence and it's something unavailable, or even unhealthy, for a middle-aged man. I then console myself with Robert Penn Warren's admonition that when one becomes an adult, "it is too late to pretend we are children at dusk watching fireflies."

Perhaps the most frightening development of becoming a grandfather is that I no longer trust time. I'm as spastic in time as Billy Pilgrim. When my oldest daughter was in the hospital having our second granddaughter, Cassie, Ellie stayed at our house for thirty-six hours or so. When we dropped her off, I wept, sobbed even, for reasons I didn't understand. My wife looked at me, wary. She knows I'm prone to clinical depression and often, even when I'm feeling good, take melancholy as a lover, at least for an afternoon, or during a soft rain, or the nights after heart-soaked holidays. But on this day, she really didn't understand. And that made two of us.

Sure I was tired—Ellie eschews sleep and likes to play all night when she stays at Nee and Pa's house—but it was more than that. Sure I was emotionally vulnerable because my daughter had just given birth to another little girl. Surely these had to be tears of joy? But I knew better. Even while crying, thoughts of my son, then twenty-seven, bubbled up from my subconscious, thoughts of all those weekends after his mother, my first wife, and I divorced. All those grim Sunday nights I dropped him at home, his real home, from the time he was two until he entered college. I'd be in nearly equal parts anguished he didn't live with me, guilty his parents couldn't stay married, relieved my diligent weekend duties were over, guilty again for that, but mainly sad that things were as broken as they were. And somehow all of that came back to me when my wife and I took Ellie back to her parents' house, not ten minutes away from our own.

My granddaughters have accomplished something believed only by certain physicists, science-fiction writers, and fantasists. They've made time travel possible. I'm living in a new world where the past, present, and future cohere and exist simultaneously. Ellie could be sitting in her high chair with Dandi and me at her side, the three of us exultant, laughing and singing, when I'm believing in the possibility of our living-room windows bursting from the sheer force of compressed joy, and in that same moment, I'll suddenly experience a paroxysm of deep regret over something I did or did not do with my own children, or of leaving my son alone with his mother. I'm suddenly hovering over the moment, levitated by grief and longing, imagining the two of them laughing; my son then looking over to where I should be standing. Sans dad. And in the next instant I'll wonder how long we'll all have each other. Will Dandi undergo another surgery or experience a second heart attack? Will we be around when Ellie's fifteen or twenty or married or a mother or a nuclear physicist? And by the time I alight back on the present, the moment I'd inhabited will be gone forever. I'm sure it doesn't help that we live in an era when the Internet seems to have flattened the globe and erased some of time's boundaries. It also doesn't help that I'm neurotic as hell. I struggle to stay tethered to the present, which is, according to C. S. Lewis, when we're the nearest to eternity.

Perhaps I need to become more like my father, who does not define himself by father, grandfather or great-grandfather. Although a loving man and a wonderful dad and granddad, he's clearly lived on his own terms. While he adores his twenty-four grandkids, he's perfectly fine letting his life remain separate from theirs. Perhaps it's the sheer number of grandchildren he has, but I suspect it has more to do with his character. There are those who act and those who worry and wonder. He also has five great-grandchildren, and when I recently asked him the name of the newest, he couldn't recall the baby's gender. The father of a good friend of mine, a Swartzentruber Amish man, has nearly one hundred grandchildren. He once told me that if he sat down with a couple of his kids and a pencil and paper, he might be able to come up with most of their names.

I realize my reaction to becoming a grandfather is not typical, perhaps not even normal. Let me assure you, it gets worse. A few confessions: I resisted getting new carpet in our library because Ellie and Cassie had crawled upon the old. I've let Ellie cover every inch of my bald pate with Strawberry Shortcake stickers. I mourned the day she stopped watching the *Wonder Pets*. I still miss Linny, Tuck, and Ming-Ming, too. I've tucked a small blanket into my belt and, having been transformed into a princess by Ellie, danced around our living room, spinning until dizzy, my blanket billowing around me like a jeweled ball gown on a hippo prancing in a field of poppy.

I want to begin saying No to the girls, but I don't trust myself. I fear that if I start I'll never stop. I'm afraid I'll say things like: don't catch the acid rain. Don't say hello to everybody you see. Don't open your heart too wide. Don't see the stars as candles in the sky. Don't feel so much. Don't see so much beauty. Don't count on anybody to be your prince or princess. Not even Pa. Somewhere along the line, your heart will break and mine will follow. At the same time I want them to embrace imagination so that, to paraphrase Wallace Stevens, the imagination can push back against the pressure of reality and help them live their lives.

I experienced none of this with my own children. Perhaps I was just too busy working and worrying about economic and marital survival to imagine time ever passing in a way that confounded me. I know I've become more neurotic and sentimental since being a young father, but that doesn't explain everything.

I want my granddaughters to "skate upon the intense radiance" of life's miracles, as John Updike once wrote in an e-mail, as he strove to catch his breath, having just come in from playing in the yard with his grandchildren. But I also want them, when the time's right, to scream the scream of No.

And this is what I mean, in part, about seeing through paradise and living in the face of the fall. Our kids are in their twenties. Our granddaughters are toddlers. Our careers are healthy. We aren't yet old. I realize that because of a recent operation and heart attack, my wife has been sick and our family life split into a before and after. I've known forever that our youngest daughter has a debilitating and progressive kidney disease, along with severe neurological problems, and that she's nearly blind and deaf, and that she's already surprised her doctors more than once with her longevity. I know my wife fears not being around to watch her granddaughters grow up. I know that we're both, maybe we're all, uncertain of the America our country's becoming, the world our world's becoming. I know all of this as surely as I know I'm living in paradise, living in the face of the fall. I'm alive in a paradise of rage and radiance, a land engulfed in love and in the knowledge that love may not be enough, a paradise of fear and the hope of wonder, as we age each new dawn and children dive into cars and drive deep into the night.

Spin Art

Brenda Miller

I'm spinning in a circle—five years old—in the backyard of that Amestoy Avenue house. Alone, save for the eucalyptus trees, still young and thin, watching in their soldierly line, and the orange trees, the grapefruit. The walnut tree too, with its fuzzy covered fruits. I'm spinning and spinning, arms flung out wide, feet in dirty red Keds, the lawn dry and almost green.

Anything that spins has, paradoxically, at its core, something quite still. Something spinning whirls in on itself, but at the same time shoots energy outward. A spinning thing—like a *dreidl*—never knows where it will land. It must acquiesce to the force of orbit. A spinning thing is isolated and connected at once.

I'm spinning and thinking of the carnival at the synagogue, walking among the games of chance until I arrive at the Spin Art machine. All the colors aligned in squeeze bottles like ketchup, while the canvas spins on its peg, so fast it's only a blur, and your job is all timing and finesse: knowing when to squirt in a bit of red, a glob of yellow. The machine itself has no intention; it's all action, all centrifugal force. "Centrifugal," I learn years later, means *to flee the center*, and that's what these colors do once thrown into the mix.

My job is patience. My job is quiet. My job is to go into the center of it without flinching, holding a color in each hand, waiting for the art to arrive. You can't see it while it's still spinning, the art hidden within motion. It will surprise or disappoint; you can't know ahead of time. Spin art is all about the unexpected. About what will be revealed once the spinning stops. Your own blueprint of the universe.

I'm spinning, and any minute now I'm going to fall down laughing, though there's no one to share the joke. But I know someone might be watching: my mother behind the sliding glass door, perhaps, or even from the kitchen, where surely she can't see me but can watch me nonetheless. Or something else—as invisible as my mother and as present—that keeps me always in sight, a force that nudges beauty out of chaos.

I'll fall down, laughing, and for a moment feel the way the eucalyptus must feel always: how movement never ceases. I'll hear the laughter of other children nearby; they're close and yet so far. All I have to do is open the gate to join them.

Any two objects that pass one another will naturally begin to spin. Here, at the Grateful Dead show, you've become a physics experiment, your body gaining momentum from each body you encounter. Bodies thin and dry; bodies heavy and damp. Half-naked bodies and bodies swathed in scarves. Bodies that have flown off their handles—arms wild, bodies unnaturally arced.

You're all spinning off one another, flinging off layers like a tire on the highway losing its tread: big hard pieces littering the road, hazardous, until you're down to bare rubber and flying. Those Sufi whirling dervishes know the most direct way in to God is via a circle—you can't get there in a straight line, as the crow flies. All this spinning shears off the crust that keeps you separate from each other, and now you're all merging until the music stops.

But even then you keep spinning, out the door to the bathroom, where all those bodies that seemed so beautiful on the dance floor now look bedraggled in the fluorescent light: lips chapped, feet filthy, pupils too dark in pale faces, skin clammy. You catch a sideways glimpse of yourself in the mirror: thin, gaunt, your hair in strings along your face—so all the treads start reattaching themselves, patching you up, re-armoring, until someone pulls you from the mirror, says gently, *don't look too long, man*. You spin back out into the crowd that's circling the stadium, a surge, and you enter that current.

Two selves: that person in the mirror, ghastly yet fascinating, and the other self merged with the crowd, without body or the concept of a body. Something you'll understand soberly years later, as you sit in a meditation group and sing the Heart of the Prajnaparamita: a chant you can't understand with your mind: *no body, no form, no tongue, no eyes, no cause of ill-being, no end of ill-being, and no path*. Then you'll walk slowly in a circle around the cushions, one foot in front of the other, a body that's constantly in flux and going away.

You'll sit in the meditation hall with a hundred others, watching the breath on its curious journey through the body, and then it will all shift: instead of you breathing air, the air will breathe you. You feel it most strongly in the gaps between inhale and exhale, between exhale and inhale, the lull at the dome of each one; you'll understand, for a brief moment, how your lungs, your heart, are ferocious—a force that has nothing at all to do with you. You'll feel the buoyancy of your heart on the repeating waves of the breath, before you come back to this solid world of the body in its habitat, the mind certain that it needs to intervene to survive.

But for now you're in this tribe of Deadheads who take LSD like medicine that might cure us of the disorder of simply being alive in the world at age twenty and twenty-one and twenty-two, the skin of our minds so tender. Afterward—*fried*: mouths dry, skin pale, shuffling these bodies that now seem heavier than before. Guzzling down quarts of orange juice to try to replenish, smoking hand-rolled cigarettes in the van, gazing out the window at the rain, the songs still unspooling in your minds—*and it's just a box of rain*—just whispers now, the rhythm beating soft in your blood.

You want only to leave this tired, so ordinary body behind: to strip away, like the eucalyptus trees you loved as a child, the way they seemed unmoved, unchanged, the row of them like sentinels against the high fence. The word "eucalyptus" means *sufficiently covered*—the buds, the seeds, the flowers—while the trunk of the tree is all about *uncovering*: stripping away. When you scrambled up among them, lifting yourself onto the berm, you found long sheets of their bark: soft and fibrous, light and heavy at once. The trunks smelled bright, fresh, as they continued to shed what they no longer need. You lay down among the peelings—your body the shape of a six-pointed star—and surrendered yourself in the slow, ponderous spin of the world.

My Heart Is a Piece of Shit

Keith Lesmeister

Low light of early evening filters through maple leaves, streams through my son's bedroom window. He's sitting on the edge of the bottom bunk. I'm kneeling next to him. He is seven and crying, tears of frustration, or anger, or both. At this point, I'm not quite sure. His hands move around his face, his hair, messy now with sweat and tears. He looks up at me—pale freckled face, one dimple, wet eyes, sandy hair—my son, he looks nothing like me. Through sobs he says, "My heart is a piece of shit."

Outside, squirrels scurry up and down the maple, their claws dig into the bark.

"Son," I say. I bring my hand around his head. This is more than scraped knees or a misunderstanding with his sister.

"I mean, crap," he says, and laughs. Snot runs out his nose. I wipe it with the back of my hand.

"What happened?" I ask.

His face scrunches. I pull him toward me so that our foreheads touch. He whimpers. "Sometimes I just can't help it," he says. He tells me that he hurt his friend's feelings by calling him names, hitting him with a lightsaber, taking away toys, and using words like *never*—"we'll never be friends again"—and repeating them, over and over, until his friend cried.

"Okay," I say, trying to think of how to address this. The truth is, I'm not sure. I've seen this behavior in him in the past; a calm calculated look flattens the expressions of his face. He does what he needs to gain the upper hand.

I hold him tight.

"It's just that I can't really help it," he tells me. He sighs. "I feel like there are two of me, like I can't control it."

And this is what gets me. Because this, for me, is familiar.

Once, when I was about my son's age, I used a wet washcloth to slap a girl's face. The girl was a year younger than I was: short, cropped hair, freckles, blue eyes. After the washcloth smacked her cheek, her eyes popped open. Her left hand covered the side of her face. She started crying. She shielded her eyes. I could already see a welt.

This girl—my mom babysat her and her older sister. I can't remember why it happened, why I did this, but even then, I hated myself for it. I felt like it was another person. Like I knew it was wrong, but I couldn't help myself.

Her sister yelled at me. Screamed in my face, "The devil is in you." And maybe that was true. I was a churchgoing kid and the notions of God and Devil were very real to me. I don't remember much after she yelled, just that I wanted to cry. For the girl, and myself; for the sense of being out of control. The feeling frightened me.

My son's tears are that of frustration. He doesn't tell me, but I know. Frustration for what you can't seem to control, but want so desperately to stop. How do I console him for a situation that I know (or hope) he'll eventually grow out of? Something he'll learn how to control through age, maturity? I tell him I know how he feels, but this response, even to my seven-year-old son, seems trite.

Outside, two squirrels squat on a low-hanging branch. It's an old, tall tree, trimmed many times. Limbs and branches have been falling into our yard. This year, certain parts of the tree will not grow leaves.

They will remain part of the whole, but exposed, bare, defenseless, vulnerable to high winds.

My son's friends are still outside, playing, and we can hear their laughing and shouting. He stands. It doesn't take long for him to realize his way out of this setback. My son—he hears his friends and what was just troubling him is lost, not forgotten, but his thoughts are elsewhere. At least for now. It doesn't take long. It never does. Moving on has never been an issue. But in the midst of these emotionally charged moments: these are my worries. For my son.

Before he runs out of his room I wrap my hand around his head one more time and pull him close. His head rests against my chest. I can feel my heart beat against his ear. I hope this means something to him; that despite our outward, physical differences, inside we are the same. I close my eyes. I kiss the top of his head, and hold him for just a second longer. He says, "Alright, Dad." And then he squirms out of my grip, dashes out of his room and down the hallway, rushing to lace up his shoes.

Truth, Truthiness, Memory, and Bald-faced Lies—and the Pleasures of Uncertainty

Michelle Herman

Let me start by telling you a secret—sort of a secret, because I've mentioned it once or twice before. But it's not something I talk about very often, because it's a little bit embarrassing. Maybe more than a little bit embarrassing.

I used to make fun of "creative nonfiction" and mock the people who wrote it. (I could say "gently mock" but I'm afraid that wouldn't be true.) Fifteen, twenty years ago, here at Ohio State, where I have taught since the late 1980s, it would not have been unusual to hear me say that if we were going to offer courses in "creative nonfiction," well, then, we ought also to be teaching "creative nonpoetry."

I couldn't understand—I would say, whenever I had the opportunity—why any writer would want to be "shackled to the truth": why he'd want to waste all that good material that might be made use of in a story.

I understood *biography*, I would say (though I had little interest in reading it—and I especially wasn't interested in the biographies of the writers I admired: I didn't *want* to know the true versions of what they'd made such good use of in fiction)—and I understood journalism, science writing, history, child-rearing guides, etiquette manuals, political diatribes. But why, I wondered, would any writer imagine that a reader cared about what had happened *in real life* to him—or her—or about what he thought about what had happened to him—or, really, what he thought about anything?

And then I started writing the stuff myself.

I didn't mean to.

I wrote my first essay a dozen years ago, after a lifetime of swearing that I never would. It was an act of desperation.

I wrote it soon after 9/11, but the essay wasn't *about* 9/11. It was about love—romantic love—a subject I had been writing about, in stories and novels and the occasional poem, for, oh, thirty years or more, if you count the writing I did when I was in my teens—and the essay was also about my daughter, who until then I had never written a word about.

It was a pretty straightforward essay: an account of things that were happening around our house just then, and of some things I remembered, *and* a direct address to my unseen audience about the meaning and nature of love and my efforts to explain it to an eight-year-old child.

And writing it was hugely liberating for me. This, as you can imagine, came as a shock.

I couldn't believe it. To plainly tell the truth, *as I knew it*? To patiently get down on paper what people who actually existed in the real world were like?—to work at getting that right and actually *know* what "right" was, instead of having to guess, instead of "right" being a moving target and sometimes even changing of apparently its own accord?

To get my*self* down on paper as accurately as I could?

To ask myself the questions, *Is this true? Did that happen?* Instead of the squishier ones, *Does this* seem *true?* Could *this happen?*

I *loved* writing my first personal essay.

And you know what I loved most of all? Getting to step out for once from behind the tree—or from inside the closet—wherever I had to hide myself when I wrote fiction (as an invisible third-person narrator, say, or behind the persona of an invented first-person narrator) and speak my mind, telling readers, for example, what it was I planned to tell my daughter when she was old enough:

> that even when love comes to nothing, love makes you *more than you were* before. Even when you know it's going to come to nothing. Even when it's just a little bit of love, a sideline-to-your-life sort of love, a temporary insanity love—a crush. Even when it's only yearning unfulfilled or half-fulfilled. Even when it comes to sorrow in the end—love exercises you. Your heart expands to make room for someone else—even if it's just for a while, even if there are already plenty of people in it. Your soul stretches and bends to accommodate the complexities of another person's soul; your mind works furiously to make sense of someone else's life and history and numerous peculiarities—and you have to be alert, you have to really wake up and listen and pay attention: you can't sit alone in your room, you've gotta come hear the music play, which you can't do sitting alone in your room with a notebook and pen thinking about your own lonely place in the universe, or rolling another piece of paper into the typewriter as you try to make sense of something somewhat related to something that happened to you or almost happened to you five or ten or fifteen years ago, or tap not quite silently on a laptop you lug along with you everywhere you go, in case you have half an hour between all the other things in your life now, trying to make progress on a novel that is, in fact, about love.[i]

Later, a writer-friend remarked that it was amazing that it took me so long to come to the essay as a writer: that it was a form tailor-made for someone as expansive and digressive (these are nice ways of saying "man, she talks a *lot*") as I. That in fact, she said—come to think of it—it was funny that I had devoted my whole life to making things up when in "real life" I was something of a compulsive truth-teller. (That's me: talks a lot and tells a lot of stories about herself, even stories that are embarrassingly personal and in which she comes off badly.)

But let me back up a little.

In the days—and weeks, and months (over a year, in fact)—*before* 9/11, I'd been working on a new novel—but like many people, after September 11, 2001, I found myself unable to continue doing what I had been doing. I had trouble simply putting one foot in front of the other, day after day. I did what I had to do—I taught my classes, I shopped for groceries and cooked meals and did laundry; I took care of my daughter. Her grandparents lived in New York City—they still do; her uncle worked in the city (and still does), and lived nearby, in New Jersey; her godfather lived in New York, too. And so her first question to me, when I told her what had happened, was about our family. When I assured her that they were safe, they were all fine, she wanted to know about the Statue of Liberty. Then she asked about the Empire State Building, and then the Chrysler Building—the Metropolitan Museum of Art, the Natural History Museum, and so on. We'd lived in the city for a year between her second and third birthdays, when I was on sabbatical from Ohio State, and we'd visited often in the years since; she thought of it as her second home, in part because it was my home.

When I finished answering all of her questions, I felt for a moment as if we—we all, I mean—had gotten off easily: it had *only* been the Twin Towers, after all. Everything else, everyone else in all the *other* buildings, was all right.

That feeling passed as quickly as it had come on.

I can't remember much about the days that followed, except for the terror (and that I kept thinking about that word, *terrorist*, how unusually apt a word it was); except for my conviction—like so many people's—that something else was going to happen, and my assuring Grace, my daughter, that nothing else *would* happen, that the worst was over. Lying, because what else was there to do? Saying what I wanted to be true—what had to be true, for her sake.

I remember that after I brought her home from school on the day itself, and after we had talked—after she asked me about landmark after landmark, and I said *yes, that's still standing*, and *yes, that too, sweet-*

heart—she spent a long time building twin towers of her own out of her quarter-inch-thick wood plank blocks—two hollow towers, as tall as she was—and then filled them with plastic Playmobil people she poured in through the open tops, and finally crashed toy planes into them and knocked them both down. Then she dug through the "rubble" to find all the scattered people. Her father and I sat side by side on the couch in the playroom watching her comb through the mountain of fallen blocks to rescue every single Playmobil person buried there and carry them off in a series of toy vehicles—not just her Playmobil ambulance, which could hold only a few of them, but her Playmobil schoolbus too, and a large plastic fire truck we'd bought at the drugstore, and a fleet of pickup trucks, jeeps, cars, motorcycles. "I can't go to bed till I find every one of them, okay?" she told us.

I remember that we watched her instead of watching the endless repetition of the crashes on TV that first night. I remember thinking that what she was doing was a lot like writing fiction, that children's play overall was really a lot like writing fiction.

While I don't remember is how many days—or weeks—it was before I sat down to try to get back to work on the fiction I'd been writing before that day, I do remember what happened when I did. I couldn't write it. I couldn't write, period. I hated the novel. I hated everything about it. The thought of continuing to work on it repelled me.

It wasn't the novel's fault. It wasn't my novel's fault, I mean. "The novel" as a concept seemed absurd to me just then: all novels, suddenly, seemed to me a folly—a sort of civilization-wide mistake. *Tell me again*, I thought, *why anyone would want to read about a make-believe person doing make-believe things*.

And day after day passed and I couldn't write. And I was forty-six years old and I had been writing just about every day of my life for thirty-nine years by then. I was at a loss. I couldn't figure out how to continue to write, but I couldn't imagine *not* writing, either. I was stuck—and oh, I was so miserable. And finally—as I say, out of desperation—and without any kind of plan—I just started *writing things down*. I told myself I would write only what was true; I told myself that what I was doing wasn't anything: it wasn't really writing, but it wasn't not writing either. It was just something to do to keep myself from going crazy.

Eventually I recovered. Like most of us. Eventually I began to write fiction again—although I never returned to that novel (I still hope I will someday—I still think I will someday, but I can't, yet; it's still too bound up with *then*). Instead, I wrote a different novel, and I published it, and I wrote a short story or two, and then I started another novel—more on that in a minute—and all of that was a relief but not really a surprise. After all, I'd been writing fiction since I was seven or eight years old. I didn't know *how* to stop. I didn't want to stop.

The surprise was that I also wrote three *non*fiction books, one after another—and that first essay, about love, was in the first of those.

The surprise was the discovery that I wasn't "wasting" material when I wrote an essay about it. I was examining it in a way I never would have examined it in fiction—where I'd "made use" of it—repurposed it, let us say. I had *always* believed that literature told "the truth" about how we are—who we are, how the world is—insofar as the writer knew it. And I had always known that good fiction creates a world that *feels* real (even when it's not *like* the actual real world—when it's a magical world or a future world—but also when it *is* like the "real world," but is not precisely *the* real word, because we have populated it with "make-believe people doing make-believe things." But for the first time, I understood why a writer—why *I*—might want to address "the truth" head on instead of slantwise; why I might want to capture on the page, instead of verisimilitude—the made-up stuff that *seems* so true—the actual, factual truth instead.

And I became very comfortable (oh, and "very comfortable" is not a place a writer really ever wants to be)—I became very comfortable with seesawing back and forth, from made-up to factual, from creating to *re*creating, from truthiness to truth. I thought I had it figured out: what one was for versus the other—I had an answer to the question I used to pose so challengingly to other writers who did both. "How do you decide what to write about in fiction versus your nonfiction?" Oh, I don't "decide," I'd say: the form makes the decision for me. If I have something to say directly on a subject—if I'm writing on a subject, or about an idea—about love, about friendship, about aging, about *American Idol*, about the unconscious—and I want to grapple with it *intellectually*, I write an essay. Simple as that.

Simple as *what*?

Ah, and this—despite the fact that I've already spent two thousand words telling you this and that—is what I started out wanting to tell you.

It's that just this past summer I discovered that what separates nonfiction from fiction for me is much more surprising than anything I'd figured out before.

In July, I was writing a section of the novel I've been working on (right now it's called *Close-Up*, but since that's its fourth working title, it may well change). I was working on a section that's set in 1979 at Yaddo, the artists' colony in Saratoga Springs, New York—a place I've spent some time myself, though not during the period I'm writing about. I suppose you could say I *repurposed* some of my own experiences in the nineties—at least, the bare-bones facts of the place, and something of its atmosphere—for the sake of fiction. As one does. (But of course I also "repurposed" some other stuff from my own life, in particular the experience I often had in my youth of becoming fond of someone of whom no one else seemed to be fond: of finding myself in the position of defender of an apparently undefendable person. [This must have had a great formative effect on me, because I come back to it again and again in fiction.])

Two of the protagonists of my novel meet for the first time at Yaddo that summer. Neither of them are versions of me, although both of them are writers—and although one of them likes the other one and nobody else who's at Yaddo with them likes him at *all*. They are a man and a woman, Martin and Jill, and they are both in their twenties and have had early success of a kind that is completely alien to me. The young man has had *tremendous* early success as a novelist—he's being hailed as the next big thing, has won a Guggenheim Fellowship and a huge advance on his new book; his first novel is being made into a motion picture—and he is a swaggering, confident fellow; the young woman, from whose point of view this section is anchored, is a poet who has won a major national prize and just published her first book. She is simultaneously socially inept and in possession of a sense of superiority to everyone around her (which is matched only by her insecurity—a paradox that I admit I did observe in many of my fellow "colonists" at Yaddo and other artists' colonies twenty-plus years ago).

Anyway: I was merrily writing away (I'm always pretty merry when I'm writing a first draft—you know the feeling, right?), day after day, all day long, living in a world of made-up people going about their made-up business, *in a real place*. I had made the decision that the artists' colony where these two characters meet for the first time wouldn't be a made-up, composite one—or an entirely made-up one—or even a real one but for which I invented a fake name . . . or, for that matter, a real *or* made-up one that I didn't mention the name of (ah, there are so many possibilities when you're writing fiction!). The decision to set a part of the novel at Yaddo, not only a real place but an iconic place—with a real history and real furniture and real gardens and real marble sculptures that I might end up describing—is notable, actually, since I'd made a decision of a very different sort about certain other places in the novel: the Midwestern city, for example, in which the poet ends up living, and in which the son of the novelist likewise ends up living—and in which a couple of the novel's other protagonists are born and raised—is never named, and that city is *something* like but is not the city I live in (the fictional one is smaller, and even more boring, than the actual one). The college where the poet ends up teaching in that unnamed middle-sized middle western city is *essentially* unnamed—it is referred to always as "State," which is the familiar, affectionate way lots of state colleges are referred to by people who assume everyone will know what they're talking about (and which I once heard someone in Columbus use to refer to Ohio State, which charmed me), and that college bears a glancing resemblance to my own, but like the city it's in is a much smaller and less interesting, much more mediocre, place. And I've made up the names of the buildings on the made-up campus, which is laid out in a made-up way, and I've made up the houses and apartments that the people in the novel live in and the restaurants and other places they go to.

A fiction writer has the freedom to do that.

So: you would think—and you will recall, *I* thought—that a fiction writer has more freedom than a writer of nonfiction. Indeed, I am going to quote myself just one more time now, from another essay. Here, I'm in the middle of my description of what took place on an evening seventeen years ago between my daughter and me.

> I don't remember what was on the stove that night—and in the oven and on the cutting board and in the mixing bowls—and I can't tell you what music we were listening to, or what we were talking about. If I were writing fiction, as I used to only do, I would be *able* to tell you. Not being able to say—having to guess, because I don't want to pretend that my memory is better than it is—is part of why I never used to be interested in writing *nonfiction*. The other part—not unrelated—has to do with what I once thought of as being "constrained by" what actually happened: stuck with and tied down by—*weighed* down by—the inartfulness of "real" life.[ii]

This is why what happened while I was working on the Yaddo section of the new novel came as a revelation to me. I was describing the poet's anxiety, her first morning at the colony, walking into the dining room full of people who seem to know one another very well. She is relieved to see that there is a table that is designated as the "silent table"—a real-life memory of my own from my time at Yaddo, and something other artists who've spent time there have talked about and even written about. Just as I did, my first morning at Yaddo, uncertain about where to sit and how to join in what seemed to be already established groups of friends, she chooses to sit there. She has brought a book, and she reads while she eats her breakfast.

I made it through this scene intact, I think (though I haven't gone back and read it yet, so who knows)—doing a pretty good job, if I do say so myself, of capturing the discomfort and self-consciousness that one associates with, say, junior high school, but that in fact never goes away—that sense that everyone else knows what to do, how to be, except oneself (Chekhov, the master, captures this precisely, by the way, in a short story called "The Kiss").

All right: later that (fictional) day, when Jill, the poet, returns to the dining room for dinner, she is dismayed that the sign indicating a "silent table" is no longer there. She hesitates at the door—everyone else is so busily knowing exactly what to do and what to say and how to be—and then she is rescued, by Martin, the novelist character who will turn out to be important in her life and in the course of the book.

All well and good.

But as I worked on that scene, I wondered about my memory. Had there been a *sign* on the "silent table" when I was at Yaddo? Or had the table been pointed out to me by someone—perhaps the person showing me around when I arrived?—who said, let's say, "This is the table for people who don't want to talk to anyone at breakfast. We know that some artists prefer not to talk to anyone before they begin their day's work." And maybe he or she had said—or maybe I had just figured out—that in the evening, after everybody's work is done for the day, there was no need for a "silent table"—that in the evening it was assumed that everyone would want to be convivial.

In the old days, I would have lost a whole day—or several days—trying to find out if there was or had ever been a sign. These days, I took to Google—and although Yaddo itself doesn't mention the "silent table" on its website, nor do any of the photographs of the dining room available online show a sign, I found my way to Google Books, where I read excerpts of a remarkable number of books that mention Yaddo's silent table. Not one of them describe a sign. Not one of them explains how anyone knew about the silent table.

And so I turned—as I ever turn, nowadays—to Facebook. My thousands of Facebook friends (feel free to "friend" me, dear reader) include many, many writers and other artists (yes, including just about everyone I was at Yaddo with all those years ago). I posted the question on my own Facebook page: does anyone who has ever been to Yaddo remember a sign?

No one did.

Everyone remembered the silent table. No one knew how we knew it *was* the silent table.

Then one of my other Facebook friends, a high-school friend, someone who I barely knew in high school but has become a frequent commenter on my Facebook statuses and photographs, responded to my question:

Can't you just say you can't remember?

And without thinking about it—as one does, on Facebook (a subject for another essay, no doubt), I typed in my own comment.

Sure I could, if this were nonfiction. But it's fiction, so I have to KNOW.

And after I hit "return" and my response posted, I paused. I thought, *Wait.* I thought, *Seriously?*

Writing about the truth, you can be uncertain. Writing lies, you have to know the truth.

And there was my revelation—my tiny, but sparkling, essential revelation:

Writing nonfiction, I could reasonably say that I remembered a sign—that perhaps there hadn't been one, but that was how I remembered it. (And it is; I do.)

I might even riff a bit about *why* I think I remember it that way—about the way "signs" appear in our memories. About the nature of memory itself. But whether there had actually been a sign or not wouldn't matter.

Why then does it matter in fiction? Why am I so sure it does?

That's easy. Because if a story is about a real place, and I mention a sign when there wasn't a sign, and the story is read by anyone who *knows* that there was no sign—or whose memory of the silent table is as certain about there *not* being a sign as mine is (or was, once) certain there was one—then the world of the novel itself comes into question: if this one thing is a lie, what else might be?

If I'm making up a sign, am I making up the people? (Well, yes, of course, I am, but once the reader starts thinking of them *as* made-up people, it's hard to take what they're doing seriously, isn't it? It's hard to believe in any of it.)

The delicate balance—between "lying" and doing everything you can to make the lies seem true, pretending with a straight face that you're not lying at all, and getting all the details exactly right so that they support all your "lies"—well, that undertaking is at the heart of writing naturalistic, realistic fiction.

What I did not understand—what I had never considered—until that breezy Facebook exchange about the sign on the silent table, was that I write fiction to explore what I know or believe to be true, and nonfiction to write about the things of which I am uncertain.

That while fiction offers more of *one* kind of freedom—the freedom to make stuff up, to rearrange and shape things into story, to take things that have happened and add and subtract from them, embroider on them, change them as much as we feel like changing them—nonfiction offers another kind of freedom: the freedom not to know for sure, and to say so. Which, paradoxically, in nonfiction, makes things feel "truer" and in fiction makes the world on the page collapse. This is perfectly counterintuitive, but nevertheless, well, *true*.

In nonfiction, even though I step out from behind that infernal tree to address my readers head-on about what I think, I am always writing what I *don't know*.

Which kind of narrative offers more "freedom"?

Six of one, half a dozen of the other.

It's no wonder I am so glad and grateful to move back and forth between them.

And really, it occurs to me now, it isn't truth or lies I'm talking about at all—it isn't truth or lies I care about. It's meaningfulness. Which we can get at either way—which we can get at in any number of ways. And I lied before when I said I was quoting myself for the last time. I'm going to quote myself one more time, because I've come to this conclusion before, even though I came to it then from an entirely different starting point.

> As I have grown older, I've found that what actually happens is at least as interesting to me as what I can make up, and that real life, when looked at closely, is enough like art that the distinction between what *is* art and what isn't is less interesting to me than it used to be. And *art* may be the wrong word. Artful might be better. For that matter, *interesting* may be the wrong word. What I mean by *interesting*, I think, is *meaningful.*[iii]

That meaningfulness—like beauty; like love—can be found in a variety of surprising places isn't news to any writer—or to any artist, working in any discipline. Or to anyone who has ever paused to register and contemplate the nature of an experience. Meaning is always available to us if we are interested in finding it, interested in exploring it. In the "truth" or in the apparent truth. In our memories. In bald-faced lies. And in the admission—even the gleeful admission—when an admission is called for, of absolute uncertainty.

[i]From "Superstar," originally published in *River Teeth: A Journal of Nonfiction Narrative*, fall 2002. Reprinted in *The Middle of Everything*, University of Nebraska Press, 2005.

[ii]From "Seeing Things," originally published in the *Southern Review*, spring 2007. Reprinted in *Stories We Tell Ourselves*, University of Iowa Press, Sightline Books: The Iowa Series in Literary Nonfiction, 2013.

[iii]Ibid.

En Memoriam

Chelsea Biondolillo

> *...how easy for us to believe in a single, concentrated cause for complexity, and how hard to find visceral satisfaction in the accretion of infinitesimal influence that is more often nature's way.*
>
> –*T. Lewis, F. Amini, and R. Lannon,* A General Theory of Love

Memories have no bones or eyelashes. They are not objects in the same way that belt buckles and tree stumps and finch feathers are. They cannot be held like prisoners or evaded like authorities. And though I like to imagine I can marshal my own, memories are biologically unreliable and behaviorally inconsistent.

As I stand on this basaltic mountain and look down the sloping green hillsides to the Atlantic Ocean, I will my mind to remember every detail of the experience. I take a quick burst of twenty digital pictures of everything I can see. I try to imprint the smells, the sounds, the way the sun feels different as it hits the Canary Islands, thirteen degrees closer to the equator than my current home in Wyoming. I'm supposed to be listening: a Spanish ecologist is giving a lecture on the anthropogenic impacts upon Europe's most diverse biogeography, but instead I'm staring down a small sparrow-like bird. It darts through the juniper bushes too quickly for a photo, so I want to memorize enough details to identify it later, when I'm back at my desk and field guides.

All day, from the top of Cruz de Taborno Mountain, to the village of Taganana at its feet, I have kept all of my senses on alert with what I hope is permanent tape rolling in the back of my brain. The lecture, the vista, the way the air smells—I don't want to lose any of it. By the afternoon, this act of trying to record everything starts to feel like a physical exertion. My brain starts to hurt, or I imagine it does. And then the worry begins, that I'll miss something, that I'm already missing something by over-thinking, that I am not in the moment. Too often, this is how my travel ends up feeling: like a race to record, rather than experience. I look around at the rest of my research group and wonder how they all manage to look so calmly engaged. They don't look like they have pained brainpans—though it's likely I'm not the only one.

A memory is an electro-chemical action. It is an *event*, like lightning, rather than an artifact. After the flash, the lightning itself only exists as an afterimage that wavers, then fades from view, leaving behind a bit of blackened wood or glassed-over sand, the smell of pennies and sulfur.

We understand memories biochemically in two distinct ways: first, as a phenomenon created, and second, as a perception retrieved. For an experience to be recorded by the brain, it must first be sensed by one or more of our eyes, ears, nose, mouth, or skin. These sensory perceptions are encoded in chemical signatures and carried by specialized nerve pathways to our cortex, then stored in synaptic neurons. For many years, neurobiologists have relied on the analogy of computer memory to describe what happens in our much more chaotic and soupy internal ecosystems. For example, a computer translates information into binary code and then stores it with address markers that will enable faster retrieval. However, the human brain doesn't generally store *information* the way a computer does. The human brain stores *meanings*: a string of numbers—0529—in a computer is data; but in my (and my mother's) brain, it is my birthday. Though two computers would store and recall the numbers identically, both my mother and I not only have different meanings associated with those numbers, they are attached to different experiences (or markers) as well. I may think about birthday cakes and parties I've had, while she may remember what I smelled like on that first day, how her body ached, the paint on the delivery room walls. Humans require a code much more complex than binary to store and retrieve our memories, a code that is subjective, errorful, and plastic in translation, as it must encompass both sensory input and meanings. And the chemistry of meaning is more art than science—we know meaning when we see it in actions, but have yet to design the perfect theory to describe it biologically.

Memories leave an afterimage of connections across the neurons in our brains, an afterimage that is only slightly more permanent than the moment it records. We must re-remember to keep most memories active, lest the connections fade. To do so, we redraw the chemical routes between perceptions and the meanings attached to them: we re-fire the lightning.

Despite my attempt to focus while on this ecology field trip to the Canary Islands, I will remember some of the things that I experience and forget others, the same way I remember some of my class periods in the fourth grade and some of the family vacations I went on as a child. My former classmates would likely remember some of the same events that I do, but even if two of us were to remember story time with Susan, our red-haired, braces-wearing teacher, it is improbable that we would describe the experience identically. One of us might still be able to hear her slight lisp, while someone else could mimic the voices she'd use as she read the book. In this case, a greater amount of data—a school year, rather than a single day—means that even greater disparity can exist between recollections.

Emotional context adds another layer to the meanings we attach to our experiences. We remember as a way to comfort fears and to confirm suspicions. Vladimir Nabokov, in his autobiography *Speak, Memory,* said, "One is always at home in one's past." This is because we can record a past that will feel like home. My little sister would surely recount our 1985 trip to Disneyland much differently than I—she being an awestruck six-year-old, I more jaded at twelve. Her father and my mother were her complete family; I was a person apart from it. She remembers a magic parade; I remember elbows in the crushing crowd. Our memories are landscaped with imperfections, gaps, and distortions, both individually and collectively.

The highest mountain peak in the Atlantic Ocean is in Spain's Canary Island archipelago. Mount Teide, or *Pico del Teide,* rises 24,600 feet above the ocean floor on the island of Tenerife with a summit peak of just over 12,000 feet. Teide's first recorded eruption was in 1396. Subsequent eruptions happened in 1430, 1492, 1704, 1706, 1798, and 1909. There was an increase in seismic activity in May 2004 and an eruption was predicted but has still not occurred. Sulfur vents near the peak are intermittently active today, and when you step off the tram that takes groups of visitors from the caldera floor to just shy of the peak, the yellow smell coats the back of your throat. The landscape remembers every volcanic event in a variety of geological and biological ways. I look out from the peak, see old craters in concentric rings of orange and gold. Past the widest ridge, the dark pine forest seems a broken, mossy belt around the island. It is easy to think of these remnants, these terrestrial memories, as more reliable than our own, but the earth, too, can seem to forget: uncomformities, missing links, and vestigial behaviors all hint at sources lost or forgotten.

Every few steps I lift my camera and snap one, two, three pictures, because I believe the pictures will help me remember better than my eyes alone will. The photos will cement only a two-dimensional view, however, not the experience. The sound of my boots on the smooth stones as I hike down under the "cloud sea," the way the breeze feels, the smell of this forest, so different from the evergreens in my long-ago home state of Oregon: all of these specificities will begin to fade as soon as I get back home and start looking through the digital files. My brain will begin to overwrite the recollection of my actual experience with the recollections stored in the photographs. It's more than just a measure of neurologic efficiency; with each re-looking, I will train my mind to remember how things looked. I will redraw the afterimage of *sight* over and over, letting the other senses go. Didn't the air taste saltier? Wasn't there a hint of flower-rot or cedar, a sweetness of some kind under the smell of pine needles?

That my own memory is fallible, as is all of ours, becomes more interesting when we try to remember something together. When we form memories socially or culturally, we call it history. And history is bound by the gaps, revisions, and rewrites of all those who would create it. Through power and agency, a subset of *we* collectively agrees on a story of the past—and without a voice of dissent, it becomes the way the past was. A truth that *becomes* as true as stones: those simpler, or harder, times gone by.

On Tenerife there is a cultural memory of the pine forest. The locals and their biographers have agreed on the way the forest was, before there were photos and surveys to attest to an informational reality. Before the Spaniards "pacified" the indigenous peoples of the Canary Islands in the late fifteenth century, it is believed that the pine forest formed a thick ring around the island, filling in the landscape from around six hundred to twenty-two hundred feet above sea level.

This vision of a stable forest before man and industry is only partially true. The pine forest was likely destroyed and recreated a number of times before the "native" Guanches ever set foot on the shores of Tenerife. The trees themselves, an extremely fire-resistant species of pine, *Pinus canariensis*, are from the Pliocene; they evolved nearly three million years ago. During the tree's evolutionary infancy, Tenerife would have still been suffering the upheavals of volcanic activity, including eruptions, landslides, and earthquakes that shaped its landscape, by both subtraction and addition. It wasn't until recently, geologically speaking, that the igneous activity on the island began to slow and invite complex biogeographies. Though Tenerife's dramatic cap, the towering volcano Teide, last erupted just over one hundred years ago, the prior ten thousand years have been comparatively quiet, allowing for the pine and laurisilva forests to root and flourish.

This is true: no human eyes saw the first pine forest on Tenerife. What we cannot know is when the first people arrived. Historians hypothesize that while Zoroaster preached in Iran and David ruled the Israelites, approximately 1000 BCE, small groups of Berbers rowed with their families, goats, and sheep from the western coast of Northern Africa to the Canary Islands. The easternmost islands of Lanzarote and Fuerteventura would prove the least hospitable—dry and hot like the coast they'd left behind—and few would settle there. But just a few more miles west, the travelers found green havens on the islands of El Hierro, Gran Canaria, La Palma, La Gomera, and Tenerife.

Records from Arab and Andalusian explorers in the first century suggest that by the time the outside world began making regular contact with the Canarian peoples, they no longer shared a common language between islands or possessed a tradition of boat-building. The Spanish conquerors were the last people to hear the languages of the islands (except for a whistling language that still exists today on La Gomera), and they documented very little of it. Agents of the crown also recorded all of the islanders as Guanche, or "sons of Teide," though the inhabitants of each island once had separate names. Guanche they all became. The people themselves kept oral histories rather than written, and no one is left who remembers why they gave up the lives of seafarers.

All those trees! Why would they give up the sea with such a seemingly endless supply of shipbuilding materials? When Europeans first began to make landfall on the Canaries, the people they found were pastoral shepherds, seemingly unaware of the great resource that belted their lands. The Guanches lived in natural caves and grazed their animals above the treeline, where there was plenty of open grassland. With the sparse record of Guanche culture preserved by early Spaniards, modern Tenerifeans cannot fully understand the nature of these early lives, what rituals gave them meaning.

Historians assume from the lack of an active naval culture that the first settlers on the islands were happy: perhaps because what came later was so devastating, we would like what came before to be idyllic. But an oral tradition preserved in fragments suggests otherwise: tales of a fiery god and his devil counterpart who lived in the belly of Mount Teide and fought for the freedom of the sun hint at ash-darkened skies and the terror of lava and earthquakes.

Droughts too were common, and when they lingered, choking the grass and drying up the springs, the Guanches would take their flocks and families to large mesas to plea with the rain gods. Once there, the lambs and goat kids would be separated from their mothers, which caused the former to cry in panic and the latter in frustration. Finally, the people would join in, entreating the sky with a human and animal chorus of despair. And yet, despite the ever-present volcano and the unpredictable rain, the Guanches existed there, in happiness or in sadness, for generations, until their overlooked resources became valuable.

I want to look across the landscape before me and see a correlative to my own memories. I want to recognize in the shapes of stony outcrops and replanted forests my own imperfect record. One is not a model for another, however; each system is fraught with a near infinite number of variables. Even the word, *memory*, seems over-simple to encompass personal *and* social *and* environmental memories. The Guanches existed and now they don't. A forest almost disappeared but has returned. I cannot stop thinking about either.

The Canary Island pine, or *el pino canario*, grows in the cloud sea, a wave-like layer of precipitation that hangs at approximately thirty-two hundred feet above sea level on Tenerife, Gran Canaria, El Hierro, La Palma, and La Gomera. The tree has a straight trunk and can grow as tall as 175 feet. It is the largest pine in the Old World. The needles are long, thin, and grow in sheaves of three. Canary pines usually have an open crown of regular, candelabra-like upswept branches, narrowly conic when young, later widening to broad ovoid-conic, and becoming irregular and dense with age. The bark is thick, fissured, and dark tan to reddish in color. Individual trees can live for six hundred years or more.

The Spanish conquest of the Canary Islands took less than a hundred years.

Different perspectives, shifting prejudices, new data—all can change how we view past events, coloring them slightly with new meaning. Just as we protect ourselves in our individual memory, so too do we protect our sense of community with our collective memories. In this regard, the land can offer a useful metaphor: as meandering rivers shift and twist their paths over the years, cutting new banks and creating oxbows, so our brain chemically recodes each memory we revisit. Over time, what occurred becomes subordinate to what we recall. We sterilize old battles; forensic historians take facts from equipment and casualty ledgers to create museum dioramas, the spears forever frozen and the blood just paint. We become like the non-geologist who sees a crater as a noun, forgetting or ignoring the terrible verb that came before.

For example, though I have tried to remember the lecture on Tenerifean land use and water rights that I heard while in Anaga Rural Park, what intrudes and insinuates is that strange little bird, the stark outline of the volcano we'd visit later that day, and a tacky reconstruction of a "native dwelling" that appeared early on the trail.

Numerous studies and court cases have found that eyewitness accounts of mundane activities are generally more reliable than those of major events. In 1986, a psychologist interviewed over forty students the day after the space shuttle *Challenger* exploded moments after take-off. He asked them where they had been and what they had been doing when they heard the news. Just two and a half years later, he asked the same students to recount their activities on the day of the disaster, and not a single remembered account matched the first. Some varied in minor details; some he described as "wildly inaccurate." Their neurons had cut new banks, and the old path was forgotten. What Freud called a screen memory—where an early event is filtered by a later one—can be used to describe the way each student's individual memory was changed in relation to the nation's collective memory of that day. So too, for the comfort of community, we rewrite our histories.

It is tough to find an early account of the Guanches that fails to mention their striking appearance. They were described by those first visitors as tall, and often blond and blue-eyed. Occasional accounts use words such as pale and beautiful. This makes some genetic sense if you take their supposed Berber origin into account.

Most modern dioramas, however, feature short, stocky characters with dark skin and black (or sometimes white) hair—closer to the oft-displayed Cro-Magnon in many natural history museums. This vision of the Guanches, which seems to conflict directly with historical reality, distracts me from my environmental studies. I can't reconcile it without bringing out a host of my own assumptions and presuppositions about conquest and the right of the victors not only to rename the defeated, but to redesign them as well—in this case, as a creature in need of evolution, not at risk for extermination.

One notable exception is outside the Basilica of Candelaria on Tenerife. Nine bronze monuments to former tribal kings stand upon rough stones facing the basilica. They are sculpted as imposing monarchs with their backs to the sea, draped in animal skins, armed. My guide raises his eyebrows when I ask why these statues look so different from the tourist displays. They look the same to him.

Not far from today's trailhead, the park service has reconstructed a Guanche cave complete with small red symbols painted outside the entrance. Our guide and lecturer explains that the symbols were maybe used to identify different tribes or even the different islands, or they might have been sigils of former *menceys*, or kings. He shrugs and then strides forward to point out an endemic *Euphorbium* plant, the cultural lecture now over.

In La Laguna, the first capital city of Tenerife, you can buy jewelry featuring sterling silver replicas of the symbols: three triangles, a spiral, a sideways *H*. Their actual meanings have been lost with the Guanches themselves, whose language, but for a few words and place names, was completely gone within one hundred years of conquest. In *A Journal of a Prairie Year*, Paul Gruchow says, "A name is not an object of substance, like a beam of light or the bud of a cottonwood or the sawing of a cricket. What makes it real is the set of associations it is forever bringing into the minds of those who hear or pronounce it." What kind of memory is this, then, when there is no more meaning or significance attached to the signifier? Are the symbols for us, the tourists, or the new Canarians?

Deep in the folds of our older, mammalian limbic brain, our emotional memory flows upon networks underneath our conscious thoughts, like the river that moves beneath a glacier. This deep memory informs our conscious thoughts, but it is not complete. Like boats left behind at landfall, narrative details that do not strengthen emotional links are discarded. For the price of comfort, we can find ourselves stranded.

It is romantic to imagine these painted and forged symbols as mementos, that they can resonate on some neural frequency too delicate to chart. But when both the recollection of the experience and the meaning are gone, what points could they plot?

In 1911, Ewald Hering, a physiologist specializing in the nervous system, observed of memory that

> as our bodies would be scattered into the dust of their component atoms if they were not held together by the attraction of matter, so our consciousness would be broken up into as many fragments as we had lived seconds but for the binding and unifying force of memory.

The fact that we have the capacity to learn and grow as people is a testament to our brain's ability to write, revise, and overwrite who and what we think we are. When we experience something or learn a new fact or skill, a flash of energy travels through our neural networks, lighting a pathway along synaptic nerves. As we practice a skill, we strengthen one pathway—carving the bank more deeply to the right or left—and as we learn conflicting or unrelated information, we weaken another. The pathways themselves don't disappear, but the routes can get broken. We forget our third-grade teacher's name, or the capital of South Dakota, when we no longer attach relevant meaning to the information.

Most pine trees have some level of biological fire-resistance. Owing to its habitat at the feet of volcanos, the Canarian pine, however, has become especially hardy. First, thick bark protects the trunk and the resin-rich heartwood from high temperatures. And if its crown is burned by windblown flames, the tree will re-sprout from buds at the base. Finally, its cones remain closed at maturity, opening only in the presence of dry heat, either from fire or drought, a trait called *serotiny.* In the absence of a fatal fire, the individual trees themselves can live hundreds of years. The pine trees store a biological memory of fire in their cells—an adaptation—and use it to propel their species forward.

When the Spanish first arrived on the Canaries they valued the human resources first and the trees second. In the late fourteenth century, merchant ships frequently visited the islands and abducted natives for mainland slave trades. But soon the land began to interest the Spanish aristocracy even more than the natives who occupied it.

Jean de Béthencourt and Gadifer de La Salle were noblemen who had sworn allegiance to the Spanish crown in exchange for rights of vassalage. The two men and their forces overpowered the sparsely populated Fuerteventura and Lanzarote islands first. The people there clung to survival tenuously in the best years, on dry land with a few goats and little else. The vassals motivated both surrenders with little more than the threat of starvation. Next, Béthencourt conquered the small number of inhabitants on the island of El Hierro, and the three islands together were considered "ruled" by King Henry III.

The natives on La Palma, La Gomera, Gran Canaria, and Tenerife resisted, however, for nearly a century. Tenerife's menceys, or tribal chieftains, held out the longest and most violently. Spanish ledgers document statistics under the term "battles," but these few place names and numbers do little to record the actual events that took place as Neolithic Guanches, armed only with spears and clubs, fought for their lives against armored Spanish musketeers and pikemen. The islanders used the steep-walled *barrancos* (wooded ravines) to their advantage. Early in 1494, they ambushed Alonso Fernández de Lugo and his conquistadors with spears and boulders, killing nearly all of the Spanish forces. They decorated hillsides with the bodies of soldiers to inspire fear in their enemy and support from their gods. This is what is remembered.

Even in imagining what those days could have been like, each of us is weighed down with our own cultural and individual memories, formed through separate processes but working together. The mind grasps at the words "native" and "conqueror" and conjures up the symbols and neural connections it has already recorded. This is a biological process that has served us well in our evolution: the ability to generalize from a few known facts. But also, thanks to the plasticity of our neural networks, we can overwrite our assumptions with experience and knowledge. This is how we grow.

On Tenerife, there is little we can experience to inform our perceptions of Guanche life: we can share a view of the landscape they once called home, trace the outline of an enigmatic shape on a mortared cave, sob at the clear sky on top of a mesa. One fact remains indisputable, however: in the first clashes on Tenerife, only one in five Spaniards made it back to his ship.

De Lugo reported back to Ferdinand and Isabella that he would not give up these lands, so fertile with labor and sugar potential, over the bodies of a few hundred Spanish men. Though he had suffered some of the heaviest losses on his first attempt to subdue Tenerife, he returned two years later, after selling his mainland properties to finance this second campaign. He brought even more men, including an unrecorded number of recently Christianized Gran Canarian tribesmen.

Eventually, the ever-renewable European troops beat the survival instincts of the Guanches. De Lugo, along with Fernando Guanarteme, a Christianized prince from Gran Canaria, completed the conquest on December 25, 1494. After the menceys Tinguaro, Bencomo, and Acaymo were one by one slain in battle, Tenerife fell. Many of the remaining natives died during the mild winter that followed, from an unknown "drowsiness" disease. Concurrent reports of Guanches running from their own dogs have led historians to suggest that a strain of rabies brought to the island with European dogs ultimately conquered Tenerife, though the Spaniards gave many decorations to their army captains.

Anthropologists have acknowledged, too, that sorrow may have played a part. The menceys must have seen plumes from the great fires that powered the sugar plantations on Gran Canaria. Missionaries from other islands were sending converts on a regular basis to speak the good word of submission to God and the Crown. On the mesas and in the barrancos, the Guanches would have understood that their time as free people was coming to a close.

Regardless of what combination of firepower, disease, and despair allowed the Spaniards to overpower the Canarians, once they had the upper hand, they kept it. While royal treaties and decrees promised fairness in land allocations between the soldiers and the natives, huge tracts were immediately seized and granted to distinguished Spaniards. The most complete record of the Guanche's treatment after the invasion is preserved in financial and legal documents maintained by Spanish church officials and government offices. Tribal leaders were beheaded, burned, or quartered based on Inquisition proceedings, or, less publicly, were delivered into the West African and European slave trades. The victors recorded that many of the island women "took" Spanish husbands, a trick of language that suggests an unlikely agency. Of the supposed fifteen thousand original inhabitants of the island of Tenerife, only nineteen were allocated property by the new Spanish government.

The memory of the land is imperfect, as is our own. As climates change and trade winds shift, forests cede to grasslands, which are then desertified. A forest may again appear in a millenia or two, but it will be because conditions were perfect for one, not because of any predetermined forest-ness to which the landscape was aspiring to return.

So too, the geologic record contains giant gaps, called uncomformities, erasures as complete as a shaken Etch A Sketch. Epochs aren't just forgotten; they are changed to sand grains and blown away. What the land saves between layers of rock is both information and context. When these layers erode, *what was* drifts as motes to collect at the bottom of a sea. We need these erasures; we cannot know everything, lest, as Ewing warns, our conscious minds be blown to dust as well.

After de Lugo proclaimed the Canaries annexed to the kingdom of Castile, after priests set to baptizing the remaining natives, overwriting their Guanche names with Spanish ones, after Ferdinand and Isabella granted the Guanche lands to European soldiers as payment for military services rendered—after all this, one tribe continued to resist. The people of Taoro, and their king, the mencey Bentor, fled to higher, undesirable ground at the foot of Mount Teide. There, the mencey threw himself off of Tigaiga Mountain in a ritual suicide, leaving his people leaderless. No one recorded how they perished.

When the Spaniards came to the islands to enslave the natives and steal their land, they did so under the guise of Christian reform and commerce. They were following an imperative of the age. This is a narrative that our collective memory has agreed upon: an apologist and heroic sense of how imperialism changed the demographics on the Canary Islands. And since the fifteenth century, historians, sociologists, and anthropologists have hypothesized and ruminated and revisited this memory so many times that it has shifted enough to now be called "wildly inaccurate" by some. How can we accept the story of the victor as historical record? Whose story do I tell when I talk about what happened on Tenerife? Without language, without tradition, without memory—what is left to memorialize of the Guanches?

To call this problem of an imperfect record merely political or semiotic is to miss the beauty of the impossibility of a true history. The problem is cultural, biological, and chemical, like memory itself.

I walk through the great desert at the foot of Teide in relative comfort, because of the nearby *guagua* (local slang for bus) and the abundant bottled water it holds. The forest is behind and below me now, over the crater edge. The ground before me is a beautiful garden of pumice and basalt formations, obsidian fissures, and an occasional dried *echium* stalk. There are some yellow grasses, and sometimes the shade of a rock tower to rest beside, but within the confines of the great crater complex, there is no river, no lake, and the porous volcanic rock absorbs the scant rainfall efficiently.

Here in the bowl of the caldera the heat shimmers over shades of black, pink, and yellow while a hot dusty wind erodes the landscape mote by mote. As we climb a vent peak, the wind cools quickly. How long the people of Taoro could live here, without water, food, or shelter, in defiance of the rule of the Crown, I cannot know.

Historical geneticists point out that the correct term for what happened to the Guanches is "assimilation" rather than "extermination." There are still traces of indigenous DNA in some of the current inhabitants of the Canary Islands. There are even small groups re-imagining the fragments of tradition into new rituals. The genes of the pine trees pass on the memory of eruption so that new trees maintain thick bark and closed cones. The genes of the Guanches might pass on something, too: something deeper than conscious experience, deeper than limbic responses. But is it the despair of surrender, or the tightness of a cone, waiting for its right time to open?

Even as the Spanish exploited Canarian human resources to near extinction, they also devoured the forests. Armies of loggers cleared great swaths of land to make room for sugar plantations, and then cleared wider to fuel them. They carved acres of sugar-cane terraces into the steeply sloped mountains to impossible heights, the shadows of which can still be seen above port towns like Taganana in the north. The sugar barons reserved lowlands for the sprawling mills and the small villages that grew up around them.

To power the mills—owned by a very few Spaniards and employing a mix of slaves, free natives, and poor immigrants who had come to the islands for the promise of land grants—round-the-clock stokers maintained enormous fires. The flames boiled the cane juice down to crystalline sugar. Workers suffered terrible conditions: burns and amputations were common, as were beatings and illnesses related to long hours breathing the smoke and processing the cane. For this, freemen mill workers received a very small percentage of the lucrative Macaronesian sugar trade. All this for less than one hundred years of prosperity: within a single century, cheaper Caribbean sugar flooded the European markets, and the Canarian mills and their broken laborers were abandoned.

The pine forest suffered not just for the mills. Homebuilders coveted the red heartwood, and shipbuilders pillaged the tallest trunks for their masts. An engineering trade boiled water-resistant pitch out of the heartwood for repair of aqueducts and ship hulls, while farmers and merchants hired women to gather the pine needles from the forest floor for agricultural mulch and packing material. From the peaks of Teide, I can see much of the forest in a single arcing glance—so too the Spaniards would have seen that the forest was as limited as the remaining Guanches. Resident merchant-run councils enacted the first forest-conservation decrees even as the Spanish government granted the first lands in 1496.

Local businessmen, however, either ignored or actively circumvented the decrees with bribes and violence against the forest guards. By the time the German naturalist Alexander von Humboldt arrived in 1799 to study the Canarian flora and fauna, he found a land substantially more barren than the one the Spanish had annexed. After the sugar bust, entrepreneurs first repurposed the cane terraces for wine, and once the market for wine dwindled, the vast steps were abandoned. From Teide, von Humboldt noticed only a few solitary trees. The deepest barrancos maintained the only traces of both pine and laurel forests by dint of the difficulty of extracting the timber once felled.

Once, our memories served us well as animals: season after season we could recall which foods were healthy and which poisonous, which areas were habitable and hospitable, whether or not another person was a friend or foe. Now, that same adaptation gives us the ability to exercise faith, hope, and charity (not to mention despair and revenge). What do I want to remember about this island, these trees, the traces of a lost history, and what will that memory serve?

On Tenerife, the people remembered the forest. As it slowly emptied of trees, the bald earth told a story of mismanagement to each new generation of islanders. They created stricter laws, heavier fines, but still the forest slipped through their fingers and into the mouths of lumber mills and the hulls of ships bound for the mainland. With the Canarian sugar and wine trades largely exhausted, the Spanish government was unmotivated to invest in the ecological plights of the islands.

In 1813 and 1841, after pressure from local economic groups, royal orders were finally made to start reforestation operations—which were then disregarded by municipal officials who complained of the expense and labor required by replanting. True reforestation wouldn't begin until mandated by the Franco regime in the early 1940s. This helped to improve horizontal precipitation (when the pine needles collect water vapor from the low clouds until it drops to the ground), and therefore productivity of the land. The aesthetic and social benefits were subordinate.

Of the five islands with former substantial pine coverage, only Tenerife maintains a percentage of original forest. I can look out from my perch on the side of the volcano and see a great belt of green—the new growth indeterminate from the old. Traces remain, in stumps and ruins, of the loss of the former grandeur, but they disintegrate even as the new forest grows around them. A modern paper on the pine forests of the Canaries called the reforestation "an example of the positive potential of human intervention in ecologically sensitive island ecosystems"—which is at once too narrow and too optimistic of a view, as a forest is made of more than just trees.

While our memories may change, our identities try to remember themselves in the ingrained patterns of thinking and doing that we revisit every day. We become who we are. When I return home, I will compare pictures with my fellow travelers. We will trade our favorites among one another, and I will see myself in their photos. Through the images, I will remember myself on this trip, in these woods. Their digital memories will augment mine. But look at a picture of yourself from childhood, even young adulthood, that you've never seen before, and it is not uncommon to experience a moment of agnosia. Without prior reinforcement, you are likely to have discarded the memory associated with that moment in time. You can look at yourself and see a stranger. You can look at a red painted mark on a cave wall and feel nothing but curiosity.

Nabokov began his autobiography with a harrowing metaphor: "The cradle rocks above an abyss, and common sense tells us that our existence is but a brief crack of light between two eternities of darkness." They had an alphabet, songs, burial rituals, and names. Many remember them as mostly nameless victims of colonialism. A very few remember them as ancestors. It is only a handful of accounts in yellowing pages and crumbling artifacts that tether what we are now to what they were then. The fragile neural networks of a scant number of scholars and activists keep a memory of the Guanches like a light. We cannot hope to account for every life lived, logic asserts.

I have these few pictures, these longs hikes up through the clouds and back down. I remember something of the trees that have returned and the volcano that yet remains; I have an idea about all that has been lost. It is, finally, a long list of information and only a guess at a meaning.

I Have This Part Right

Penny Guisinger

In the dark of a February evening, people danced in the street. I was maybe eleven years old, watching them through the windshield of my parents' car. My memory has it all wrong, I know. I was in the front seat with my mom, and we were parked right at the edge of the circle of pavement where people were swinging each other to the music and laughing. Snow collected on their shoulders and in their hair. That can't be right. Daddy was somewhere else—I picture him in a store, but he had been in there for a long time, engaged in one of the lengthy, rambling conversations that were his trademark. Mom stared hard out the windshield at the people dancing. She was young, in her twenties, and her face was lit only by the dashboard lights. Her long, straight brown hair draped over her shoulders, and her fingers were wrapped around the steering wheel. She was waiting. Was it really snowing? She looked at the crowd, looking for my dad. In the darkness of the car with the engine running, we had the heater on. She said, "He knows I love to dance."

The threat of my parents' split was a strong scent that wafted through my childhood home, and I feared it—like smoke from a chimney fire drifting down through the rafters. "Are you going to get a divorce?" It must have been shocking for her to hear this blunt question—like a blast of hot flame.

I have this part right.

"No," she answered. She put the car in reverse, and we backed away from the street dance. The music and the lights receded in front of us in the swirling, falling snow. "You don't need to worry about that."

❖

I had plenty to worry about during the five-day hospital stay that followed the birth of my son, Owen. He came into the bright lights of the operating theater through a wound cut into my gut by a scalpel, and my recovery was complicated. The pain and the drugs and the hormones and the overwhelm of a new baby combined to make me cry for hours at a time. My husband, John, disappeared for hours at a time, took himself and his book and his sketchpad down to the cafeteria or out to a coffee shop, so he could relax while I cried and nursed and watched television.

Hours after the surgery I refused more narcotics and tried to make it on Tylenol, because I didn't want my son to absorb painkillers through my breasts. Deep in the night, I awoke to the wetness of my own tears and sweat soaking the pillow. The pain was too much.

The doctor said, "Don't be such a hero."

My husband slept, peacefully tucked into the second bed in my hospital room.

The next day, he lay stretched out on that bed, flicking through channels on the television. One hand tucked beneath his head, arm out, elbow bent, the other hand holding the remote, while on my own side of the room, I cried hard beneath the white, cotton hospital blanket. Tears landed on our newborn son, sleeping up against my breast.

"You know," he said, his eyes still on the television, "you bring a lot of this on yourself."

❖

My daughter was six years old when a therapist taught her how to act like a turtle.

"The idea is to teach Abby how to give herself some space," the therapist said to me in the waiting room of the community health center. It was a narrow room. At one end, a collection of toys—a plastic kitchen, a bin full of action figures with missing limbs—waited for someone to play with them. "She needs to learn how to take herself out of a situation. To collect herself."

I had started bringing her to therapy when her anger had become pervasive and undeniable. When faced with the smallest slight, the tiniest reprimand, her face assumed a deep scowl—forehead furrowed beneath brown curly hair, mouth pressed into a hyphen, green eyes cold and narrow—and she stalked off to stomp and slam doors. She was a tiny-fisted, furious force in the home we now shared with Kara, my new partner.

And so she was instructed to be a turtle when she got angry. She was instructed to go inward—retreat into a shell—when she felt her anger get out of control. By being a turtle, she might survive my divorce. She might also survive whatever humiliations were sure to come from being in a small town and having her mother leave her father for a woman. She might survive my selfishness.

I drove her to counseling every week for a year. I drove her through all weather, through the darkest New England nights to these appointments. The drive took an hour each way. We went on Tuesday nights, while her dad was practicing with his band.

Sometimes I dropped her off and tried to squeeze in grocery shopping or some other errand. Sometimes I brought a book and sat in the waiting room, trying to read. Sometimes I brought four-year-old Owen, and we went to McDonald's for a fruit cup or a carton of chocolate milk. He would slide into the bright red booth and talk his incessantly cheerful talk. I leaned gratefully into his company. Always I spent that fifty minutes worrying about what was going on in that room with the puppets and the sand tray. What maternal crimes or shortcomings were being revealed?

She practiced being a turtle in the grocery store one day as the sliding glass doors whooshed shut behind us. She was angry at her little brother, and I watched her take herself to the far end of the store, near the meats and pickles, to collect herself.

I shopped for vegetables and bread, but kept an eye on Abby. I put broccoli and strawberries into my cart while watching for her girly, purple coat and lavender boots. She stayed within sight—but kept herself apart—stayed inside her shell. Owen stayed next to me, held onto the cart, and narrated the items on the shelves. Cereal. Syrup. Bread. We moved from aisle to aisle, and Abby appeared, dutifully, at each far end. We moved in orbits.

I wondered, "Is this parenting?"

A few days later, I sat across the table from Abby's teacher, Ms. Higgins, clutching that day's note in my hand. *Abby got nothing done today. She sat at her desk scowling and refusing to do any of her work. She lost both recesses. We need to talk.* In spite of the histrionic notes she sometimes sent home, Ms. Higgins was exactly the right person to teach kindergarten and first grade. She was a blend of kindness and clarity, softness and boundaries. Tall and super thin with short graying hair and thick glasses, she wore wool cardigans and slacks. She had called me in for an afterschool conference.

The miniature chair I sat in folded me up so that my knees were abnormally close to my chest. It felt like my body was being rolled up into a protective ball, my limbs and head pulled into a shell.

"I don't know what to tell you," said Ms. Higgins, her hand resting on an example of Abby's unfinished schoolwork. Her finger tapped the blank spaces next to the drawings of cats and trees and rocket ships—empty lines where there should have been awkward, child-written nouns. "She gets this scowl on her face, and I can't reach her." She looked me directly in the eye. "Is something going on at home?" I had brought this, too, on myself. On both of us.

I imagined writing a note back. *Dear Ms. Higgins, Please excuse Abby from spelling class today. Her life has been ripped in half and she's not feeling well. She's learning how to be a turtle. I am told it will help.*

❖

I have rituals that help. When I board a plane, for example, I walk through the hollow limb of the airport knowing that I will die, that the plane will plunge from the sky in a fiery ball unless I take certain steps. The first step is to always—always—run my hand along the smooth, curved steel of the fuselage as I'm stepping on board. I press my hand against that thin shell of metal, relishing the glossy enamel paint. I will it to keep its perfect arc. Once on board, I set out to find my person. On every flight, there is someone—someone I can pick out on sight—who would obviously never, ever, under any circumstances, die in a plane crash. A mom with kids. A college-aged male athlete in need of a haircut. A black man with a beard and glasses. Notably, it's never me.

Then I break a Xanax and swallow one of the half-moons. The pill sands the ragged edges off, but I don't sleep. I am too busy watching the faces of the flight attendants for any sign of hidden panic, watching them push the awkward drink cart down the aisle, accepting people's empty plastic cups and crumpled napkins, watching to see if they have picked up their pace, if they know we're already on our way down. I measure the speed with which they reach out and pluck peanut bags off trays, watching for haste. I am very busy on the plane.

❖

I could have used a ritual the day I moved out of my house. The truck I borrowed from my boss was loaded. Half the dishes, half the books, all my clothes, half the toys—the shock absorbers sagged. There was no room for the kids. I was moving only twenty miles away.

We made a plan: my ex would deliver the kids to my new home that same afternoon.

But Abby didn't understand the plan, though I had explained it using words from a book about divorce. "Mommy and you and Owen are going to have a new house. It's going to be fun." She understood, but when she saw me climbing into the driver's seat of a truck packed with my belongings, she screamed. She screamed, "Don't leave me," as I started to get behind the wheel. I reassured her. Cheerful as I explained the plan, I told her not to cry. "This is going to be fun!" I started to drive away, but the sound of her begging rang in my brain, and I stopped the truck midway down the driveway. With all ten fingers wrapped hard around the steering wheel, I cried gasping sobs—I froze there for what felt like hours—then I drove away. I stuck to the plan.

I have made mistakes. That was one of them.

❖

Six inches long, brown-bodied, lemon-colored spots—the salamander was the biggest I had ever seen. We found it next to our driveway on an early spring day. It was resting in a pool of water, about eighteen inches deep, on brown, waterlogged leaves.

Abby leaned over for a closer look. Her face came close to the water's surface. "Do you think it's dead?"

We had been living in our new home—the home of my new partner—since the previous autumn, and had taken to the practice of walking on the weekends down our half-mile long driveway. The dirt road rose and fell, winding its way through thick woods. Trees pressed in against the margins and shaded the way.

I poked lightly at the salamander with a long stick, and it wiggled in response. I fished it out and let it rest on the palm of my hand. Its skin was firm and slick like a sausage casing. We took turns holding it, touching it, turning it over to see its belly. It seemed sluggish and cold, as if it had just woken up from a sleep about the length of a winter. Once we had thoroughly examined it, we returned it to the watery hole. It swam purposefully back to the leaves at the bottom and hunkered down.

This pool of clear, spring water was held in a round slice of concrete pipe about two feet tall. It was there, sitting on its end, collecting leaves, sticks, and rainwater, as it had been for an unknown number of years. It could have been a discarded piece of culvert. It might have been a cast-off remnant of someone's septic system. How it came to live next to our driveway was a mystery.

I felt uncertain about leaving the salamander there. The concrete walls were slick. I wondered if it could climb out, and if we were missing an opportunity to rescue it. I made the decision to leave it alone. This was another mistake. There were so many across this time. As I parented this complicated girl (and her less-complicated brother, who sometimes seemed, even at just four years old, to be parenting me right back) I often wished for a set of airplane-like rituals to help me through. A thin, arced fuselage, a lucky person, flight attendants to study. Some bearer of news from the future, even the near future. News from the following day or week would have been enough. Some reassurance that we would make it past even the very day we were in.

Abby's therapy sessions had, over the winter, focused on the dueling themes of loss and control. "This is who she is," the therapist explained to me under the sickly fluorescent lights of the waiting room. "She would have had these issues even if you didn't get divorced. Abby needs to be in control or she's not happy." She had paused to make a note to herself on the outside of the folder containing Abby's records. "But, yes, your divorce has probably deepened the problem."

Owen, through the miracle that is gender or personality or placement of the planets when he was carved out of my body, was not plagued by the same anxieties as his sister. He slept better, ate better, cried less. While Abby had depended on a pacifier for comfort until the age of five, Owen had never taken to the vice, and if I ever managed to coax one between his lips he would spit it out, offended. I sometimes envied him his cool outlook, his reassurance. My lack of these things were my gift to my only daughter. I had hoped to do better, to gift her with self-esteem and a confidence bordering on self-righteousness, but since I didn't have those things either, I would have had to conjure them from the air and snow. I found, across this time, that I wasn't powerful enough.

We walked back to the house, leaving the salamander where we had found it.

Two days later, on another walk, we returned to see how the creature was faring. Peering down through the water, we saw it there—just where we had left it—lying on its bed of slowly dissolving leaves. I nudged it with the stick. It did not wiggle this time, instead drifting stiffly off the leaves. It floated for just a moment, then landed on its side, its body now rigid. Legs, tail, and toes were splayed and inelastic.

Abby took a breath next to me. "He's dead," she half-whispered.

Fishing the small corpse out of the water, I let it rest, once again, on the palm of my hand. The color of its skin had shifted from its previous rich, mocha brown to a color with shades of plums or eggplant. Its spots had faded and were now the color of dust.

"It's not the same one," Abby said. "It's a different color. This one is purple. The one we found was brown."

Her face was solemn, forehead knotted fiercely in concentration as she crouched next to me, studying the tiny remains in my hand. Coat open in the front—zipper dangling down and touching the slowly thawing ground, she was dressed for this early March day. Her pink, striped fleece hat was shoved down over her ears, brown curls escaping around the edges. Underneath her rubber boots, the frost on the crisp grass was yielding to the warmth and softening.

"You don't think it's the same one?" I asked her, uncertain, once again, of the best position to take.

She studied it for a moment longer. "It's a different one."

I considered this possibility while I thought about the moment that I had released this doomed animal into the frigid water in the concrete circle two days ago. I wished I had listened to the usually-wrong voice in my head when it wondered if this salamander might appreciate being placed, instead, on the ground. There were so many mistakes.

"I guess it's possible," I answered her, turning the creature over. Its belly was darker too. Was the water too cold? Were the sides too slick to climb?

We left the dead salamander under some ferns next to the concrete tube and the water. As we stood and walked away, I considered doing what so many parenting books say to do: tell her the truth. Instead I said, "I wonder what happened to the brown one." If I couldn't conjure the magic it would take to create a better world for her, I could at least protect her from this one.

She shrugged and kept walking, kicking at rocks with the toe of her pink rubber boots. The rocks skittered ahead of us.

When we entered the house, Abby immediately told Kara what had happened. "The salamander was gone," she explained, peeling off her coat and hat and letting them drop to the floor. "But there was a different one there, and it was dead."

Kara gave me a look that asked all the obvious questions. *Why don't you step up?*

I busied myself untying my boots rather than meeting her eyes. Everyone is a parenting expert, I reminded myself, until they become parents.

I heard her say, "That's so weird, Abby. What do you think happened?"

Abby shrugged and scampered up the stairs. I sat, boots now off my feet, staring at the floor. Kara crossed the room toward me, without speaking, and briefly put a hand on my shoulder.

Outside, it began to snow.

❖

I was the kid who could never stay for the whole slumber party. The kid who couldn't make it through a week of summer camp. The kid who had to be picked up by her mom. I would awake amidst the heap of my girlfriends, their bodies and sleeping bags and pillows and long hair all an indiscernible jumble in the dark, and start to cry. The evening of truth or dare and plotting to immerse each other's fingers in warm water and séances took some kind of toll on me, and I felt alone and unnoticed there among this pile of girls. I knew that my parents, by this time, were expecting the call, and I made it. One time, at Julie's slumber party, I didn't tell anyone I was leaving, and the next morning, Julie's dad did a head count to find that one was missing. "She went home," Julie told him. I imagine her barely looking up from Monopoly. It was expected. The camp director expected it too, by the third summer, and when I appeared in the door of his office one afternoon, he said, "Time to call your mom?" Nobody tried to talk me out of it. My homing device was on and beeping, and I just needed a ride.

I wonder now if I was trying to get home to prevent something bad from happening. Something completely out of my control. In my memory—which continues to have things completely wrong, I know—I was the sun to the family's orbits. I thought I was the center of gravity. In my absence, everyone might spin out into the vast nothingness of the universe.

❖

John and I tried to make the first Christmas as normal as possible. I moved back into my old house for three days. I bought all the groceries and did all the cooking and wrapped all the presents—too many—and piled them up, around, and under the tree. I made cookies. I made fudge. I hung stockings and lights. I put big bows on packages. I put green and red glitter in a bowl of oats and we put it outside for the reindeer. After making sleigh tracks with a two-by-four outside my former front door, I spilled the sparkling oats onto the surface of the snow.

I slept on a camping pad in my former dining room.

After Santa had come and gone and the holiday was over, it was time for me to go home, to go back to how things really were. We let the kids choose which toys were to live in which house. I took the kids with me, and we left half of their new toys behind. They were sad and whining. I reassured them cheerfully that they would be back at Daddy's house in just a few days.

As I got into the car, I pressed my palm against the smooth curve where the door meets the roof, and held it there, willing it to fly, to keep us aloft. We all drove away.

❖

The year I turned forty-three brought mysterious medical challenges. I offhandedly mentioned some persistent chest pain to my doctor one day, and was handed a fast ticket to the emergency room. This led to six months of stress tests, x-rays, monitoring of my cardiac enzymes. I learned a dictionary's worth of new vocabulary: PVCs, bradycardia. I learned how to spell arrhythmia. The first cardiologist I saw proposed entering my heart and zapping the offending cells into oblivion. The diagnosis in the end? Anxiety.

The wheezy breathing brought on by cold air for many years evolved into full-on asthma that year, and I had to remember to carry a red plastic inhaler everywhere I went. It made the daily mental checklist: car keys, wallet, laptop, inhaler. What exacerbated it in a way that no amount of cold air or exercise or dust particles ever could? Nerves.

I developed a rash on my face. Sometimes pimply and scaly, at other times blotchy, under my nose and on my chin and next to my eyes. It would spread up both cheeks sometimes. "It's eczema," my doctor said as she wrote me a prescription for steroids. "Stress."

I tried to stop taking antidepressants, after having them in my bloodstream and my brain for years. As I cried my way through the first two days, I worked to convince myself that this depth of what I called "honest feeling" was healthy. Then the wave broke over me and my depression tied itself to my wrists and ankles—anvils. It moored me to a spot deep on the floor of the ocean and I could barely see light. "Don't be such a hero," said my doctor.

Anxiety is all carnival mirrors and prisms—those mirrors that make thin look fat and fat look fatter, that flip things upside down and insert twists and loop-de-loops, complete with calliope music in the background—the creepy kind. Refracted light, reflected images. It's my brain playing card tricks on itself—pulling itself out of a hat by its own ears. It's never knowing if the ground I'm stepping on is really going to support my feet, but it's not like I get to stop walking. It's always looking for my person, looking for a hard fuselage to put my hand on, getting ready to fly.

❖

It made me angry, all the time, to live with him. It made me bitter, all the time, to talk to him. Watching him walk away from me, over and over, made me smoke and drink too much. There wasn't enough therapy or antidepressants in the world to make me love him. I tried too hard. I stayed too long.

I bought a book called *Good Parenting Through Divorce*. The preposition made me laugh out loud. It reminded me of titles like *Sexy Thighs Through Running*. Define it either way—it still works.

Telling myself that I was staying for the children worked until I realized that someone languishing in a loveless, sexless, emotionless marriage was a poor role model. I considered this one day while I watched my husband patch the hole in the wall created when, in the middle of an argument with me, he had hurled a guitar stand. It had penetrated the sheetrock and stuck there, like an arrow. I was complicit, for I had goaded him. I knew where the buttons were.

His hand moving slowly across the surface of the sheetrock, he said, "Love shouldn't be like this."

Good parents sometimes get divorced.

❖

Abby was crying. Her knees were scraped and bleeding. She had dirt on her T-shirt and shorts, and more dirt ground into her elbows and shins. She had twigs and sprigs of cedar in her hair. She came into the house like this, crying, and holding onto Chloe's leash.

The dog had a half-dozen porcupine quills sticking straight out of her nose, like the prow of a ship.

Just before Abby turned eight, Kara and I had adopted Chloe. She was a mix of who-knows-what—maybe collie and retriever, with a brindle coat. She had been abandoned by her former family. They moved away and left Chloe and another dog tied to doghouses in the yard of the now-empty house. A neighbor noticed, and the dogs were rescued. She was fostered in a rescue home, and then came to live with us.

The day of the porcupine incident, Abby had been walking Chloe on a leash down our road. As I wiped the dirt and the rocks from her skin with a warm, damp cloth, Abby told me that they had come across a porcupine off in the trees, and Chloe had run after it. She told me, through choking sobs, that she had not let go of the leash, but instead had fallen and been dragged across the driveway and into the woods. I put brightly colored Band-Aids on her knees while she begged me not to let Chloe die.

She stood next to me, hovering, while I crouched on the kitchen floor and used pliers to pluck the small quills from the dog's snout. They came out easily, but dripped small drops of blood on the linoleum. Chloe barely flinched.

As I held Abby afterwards, as her breathing returned to normal, as she recounted the story over and over, she kept saying, "I didn't let go of her. I was too afraid to let go." Abby thought she was the gravity that held Chloe to us. This required her constant attention.

Over the course of a few weeks, Abby's level of worry about Chloe landed us both back in the low-slung community health center for weekly counseling. She was waking up in the morning, gripped with fear that Chloe had somehow disappeared while she was sleeping. On the nights that she spent at her dad's house, she would begin and end every phone call by asking about Chloe. "How is she? Where is she? What is she doing? Can you put her on the phone? Don't let her run away."

The counselor gave us instructions for making a worry jar. An empty jar, with a lid, filled with water and some glycerin, the worry jar was a place to store the things that made Abby nervous. She was taught to open the jar, and think about how many things she was nervous about. ("Nervous" became the code word for "anxious." "Nervous" was easier to explain to Abby than "generalized anxiety disorder.") Abby learned to shake glitter from a container into the jar—the number of shakes equaled the number of nervousness-provoking thoughts. She then put the lid back on, shook up the jar, and watched her troubles swirl around, glinting and reflecting light in the viscous water. This child-sized form of meditation was supposed to help, even though I never quite got the ratio of glycerin to water right, and the glitter had a way of clumping up at the top. Abby's small hands were challenged to screw the lid on tight enough to keep all the water inside, so shaking it always involved some amount of leakage. Somehow, this seemed to help.

I secretly wished for a worry jar that I could use. How many shakes of glitter does it take to represent the worry of ruining your only daughter?

❖

Before I moved out, I called my mom. I needed her permission to do this thing. I needed her endorsement of what I was about to do to Abby and Owen. I assumed she wouldn't like it, wouldn't sign off, would say something like, "I think that's going to be really hard on your kids." She had stayed, and I assumed she expected the same of me.

"I can't stay here," I told her. "What would you think if I moved out?" I twisted my fingers up in the phone cord, ready to endure a long pause, ready to wait.

She said immediately, "How can I help?" There was no wait.

I thought of her making the decision to back the car up, away from the dance floor, and remembered that I had imagined the snow. It was the trick of carnival mirrors that made me think she did not have my resolve.

❖

After a year had passed, we started inviting John over for dinner now and then. We would spend a relatively comfortable evening around the dining room table, and I always drank too many glasses of wine to help me through it. But the kids loved it, loved having us all together, loved having their broken family repaired for at least a few hours.

Always, when the time came for him to leave, Abby stationed herself at her bedroom window to watch until his taillights disappeared behind the pines, and I had to hold her while she cried herself to sleep.

The book about parenting through a divorce didn't tell me that would happen.

It also failed to use these words: shared custody means signing away half of their childhood. That my friends, in an effort to "not take sides," would work to become much closer to John than they had ever been before. That whatever my kids needed—a specific pair of shoes, a book, a Lego piece, a DVD, a doll, a sweater—would forever be at the other parent's house. That their very best drawings and paintings could only appear on the fridge at one house—that we would negotiate over these artworks. That not one single registration form in the whole world—for dance class, for violin lessons, for therapy, for admittance to the emergency room, for book orders—acknowledges that kids might have more than one address and phone number. That my kids would learn that the phrase "I wish you and Daddy still lived together" would become the fast, direct road to extra television time, more sugar—whatever they wanted.

The parenting book made it sound like the challenges would all be internal, invisible, and my job was to ferret them out. The book made it sound like this happened all the time and that resilience was the only key. What the book left out was any consideration of the resilience of parents. There was no chapter on coping mechanisms for people like me. I had to write that chapter myself, and I did it every day, every time I counted to five over and over to calm myself or imagined writing scathing letters to the editor of the book about divorce. "This isn't as easy as your book made it sound," I imagined typing to the smug author. "My kids are probably going to be fine, but the effort might kill me. Why didn't you write about that?"

❖

I held the newborn rodent curled in the palm of my hand. Its almost microscopic toes were tucked under its chin, and it was bucking and squealing. With my other hand, I was working fast to pluck angry red ants from its soft, newborn fur—barely discernible from its soft, newborn skin. There were at least a dozen ants, biting and crawling in and out of the small folds made by the mouse's bent limbs. Before I tossed the ants into the grass, I savaged each by rolling it hard between my thumb and forefinger. Their legs, pincers, antennas, and firm bodies all balled together for just a moment before they became airborne. These vicious, well-organized minions were working to rip the newborn to pieces, and even as I worked to prevent that from happening, I wondered what the point was. My own shortcomings were so clear to me by this time that I had no illusions I could change what was inevitable for this mouse. I could barely get my own babies through childhood intact.

Kara had found the mouse in the grass, next to the garden, abandoned by its mother and in the throes of dismemberment. I had swung into action because I needed to do right by somebody's babies, even if I couldn't get it right for my own. Those ants were easier to crush than the things I feared were eating my up own kids. I could do this even if it didn't ultimately matter.

Once all the ants were removed, the animal stopped its tiny screams and relaxed into the folds of my palm. It was a mouse. Or a shrew. Or a vole. We had no idea, really, what kind of animal it was, how many days ago it had been born, or where its mother had gone. It lay there panting softly. Its eyes were clamped shut, too young to know daylight from night. We stood there, under a sinking July sun, next to tomato, kale, pumpkin, and chard plants—the rims of the leaves were lit from behind and shone like medals. We stood together, looking at the mouse, knowing full well it would die.

The area around our garden was lousy with tiny red ants, and they would immediately find the mouse again if we put it back in the grass. If the mouse's mother was going to come back, she would have done so by now—she would not have given the ants enough time to swarm. I had tried, twice in the past, to feed abandoned baby mice through trimmed-down eyedroppers. Neither baby survived, and I had learned that a human can't replace a mother mouse. Even if I got in the car, made the trip to the store to buy a can of kitten milk, trimmed the eyedropper in exactly the right way, held the creature just so, and coaxed the life-giving fats and proteins into its mouth—it would die. Probably right there in my hand.

And there was Abby to consider. She was due to arrive from her dad's house the next morning. She was too keen, her senses too sharp, for me to keep such a secret, and if she saw it, saw me feeding it, she would become attached. There would be no way to craft a salamander-like lie around this one. She would be there, watching it die, right next to me. And all of that, all the wasted time and gas and energy and tears, when the outcome was certain—what was the point? I was learning, or trying to, that there was relief in knowing my own limitations, the edges of my power. There was, somewhere, a list of the things I could fix, and this was not on it.

We made a nest out of a bowl and some hay and left the mouse in the garage overnight. We hoped it would be over in the morning.

It was not over in the morning. The mouse was exactly as we had left it: breathing, snuffling, warm, and entirely alive. We left it there in the garage while we went about our morning routines. We made coffee. We listened to the news. My kids came back from their dad's. After getting out of his car, they walked right by the garage, blissfully unaware. I checked on the mouse now and then as the morning went by. I thought about different ways to die. I had heard that starving to death is painful, but that drowning can be worse. I wondered what it would be like to be crushed under the giant tire of a car. Would it be too fast to hurt? Was that possible? I thought about mercy and what that really looked like.

Kara and I stood in the kitchen, trying to decide what to do. Somewhere in the house, the kids were playing. I heard their laughter, their thumping noises. Kara pushed a strand of hair out of my eyes, and I straightened her glasses.

The right thing to do was to kill it fast. It was peanut-sized—fragile and soft. It barely had bones to break. I tried to place it on the continuum of the animal kingdom closer to insects and further from myself and my kids. I searched the area behind our garage—the place where we stack our wood and store our bikes—for some tool to do this job, trying dissociate from its aliveness. I tried to think of it as a plant or a larval mosquito—something operating purely on genetic programming. Nothing that would be missed. I stepped over a pile of boards and thought about using one: flat and hard. I looked at our woodpile—each piece of firewood had an end that was flattened by the chain saw. Any one of them could do it. I tried to picture each item as it would look after I was done with this task. I pictured the blob of red and fur that would smear across any of these surfaces. It had to be something that I didn't have to clean off.

I saw the cinder block at the base of the woodpile.

Something took over. Some sort of focus—a certainty. I wasn't gifted with any sort of moral quiet. No voices spoke to me saying, *you are merciful, you are kind, you are sparing this animal a much more painful end*. What seized me was closer to the feeling of a deadline. The feeling that something has already gone on too long. The feeling that, even though I did not bring this situation on myself, it was mine to manage, like so many other situations I was in. There were so many bad decisions I had made, so many wrong turns, so much damage that I believed I was inflicting—I had to do this right. And it had to be now.

One-handed, I lifted the cinder block, walked behind the woodpile, placed the mouse on a flattened spot on the ground, raised the cinder block in the air, and brought the flat side down on the mouse as firmly and decisively as I could. I then stepped on it, pressing it further down with my boot. All these steps—the walking, lifting, crushing, killing—felt like one singular motion. One smooth, hard decision.

I lifted the block slightly, needing to know if I had finished the job. Even if this turned out to be the wrong thing to do, I needed to know that I had done it right. The mouse was there, surrounded by a halo of red and wetness. I dropped the block again and staggered out of the shed into the sunlight. The shock of what I had just done pressed in and made me dizzy.

Abby emerged from the house and ran across the lawn to me, her brown curls bouncing. She was long-legged and smiling. Her arms, lithe and tan, wrapped around my waist. She leaned her head against my chest. I felt her warmth and let the light of her smile into my body, let it put my legs back underneath the rest of me. I felt the shaking subside.

❖

When the puppet show was over and we parted ways, Abby stood next to my car, watching her father and his new girlfriend walk across the parking lot. She stood, motionless, and watched them get into the car—watched the headlights flick on—heard the engine start. She stood there, in the darkening, thickening evening summer fog, in the grass with thick coastal dew already collecting on its tips, and watched. She wore her winged unicorn costume. Its hood, the unicorn's head, covered her own. From behind, I watched this small, fuzzy, hooded girl with crinkly, iridescent wings, with ears standing up on top of the hood, with the horn pointed toward the tree tops, as the night started to get dark. She had two blue balloons tied to the zipper of her costume, and they floated silently, not moving, just above her unicorn's horn. I could not see her face. That picture, of this small, shimmering unicorn, standing stock-still with unmoving blue balloons over her horn, serves up evidence of our failures. Her grief bobbed above her head next to the balloons in the blue light of dusk as she watched her father's car pull slowly away. The trees and grass and asphalt and sky became bluer and bluer as the minutes passed. I tried to coax her into my car, but she wanted to watch until she couldn't see his car anymore. She wanted to watch us move away from each other.

When she finally allowed me to talk her into my car, she became a weeping, devastated unicorn with blue balloons, and as I drove us home through the cobalt fog, my hands gripping the wheel, straining to see the road, I wept too. It was one of those foggy nights when putting the headlights on high didn't make the route home any clearer. We all drove into that fog.

Our driveway is a long, wooded approach. It's several minutes of gravel under the tires, trees lining both sides of my peripheral vision, and then the house appears at the far end of the clearing. In the dark and fog of that night, it was just a large, black shape. There was a single light left on in an upstairs window—Abby's room. She had left on the daisy-shaped lamp that served as her nightlight. Made of molded plastic, it had pink, bulbous petals and a perfect green circle in its center. The daisy was intended to hang on a wall, but we kept it on the windowsill instead, leaning against the glass. That night, from across the field and through the fog, it appeared to us as a glowing, pink flower floating two stories up in the night.

I heard Abby humming a song behind me. I have this part right.

We drove toward that light.

Contributors' Notes

Marley Andino

Marley Andino is a Virginia-based writer and sculptor. "Fish" is an excerpt from *Dry Land*, her recently completed memoir about one unforgettable winter spent traveling both sides of the Mexican border. She is currently at work on *Lamb*, a collection of essays about her childhood on the Chesapeake Bay.

Chelsea Biondolillo

Chelsea Biondolillo is currently writing somewhere out West, having recently completed an MFA in both creative writing and environmental studies at the University of Wyoming. Her prose has appeared or is forthcoming in *Shenandoah*, *Passages North*, *The Fourth River, Hayden's Ferry Review*, *Flyway*, *Brevity*, and others. She is currently at work on a book about vultures that combines memoir, travel, ecology, and history with a lot of beautiful birds and dead animals. Chelsea is originally from Portland Oregon, and rain is a frequent figure in her dreams.

Christopher Bundy

Christopher Bundy is the author of the novel *Baby, You're a Rich Man* (C&R Press, 2013). He lives in Atlanta, GA.

Steven Church

Steven Church is the author of *The Guinness Book of Me: a Memoir of Record, Theoretical Killings: Essays and Accidents*, and *The Day After The Day After: My Atomic Angst.* His fourth book, *Ultrasonic: Soundings* will be released in 2014 by Lavender Ink. His essays have been published or are forthcoming in *Brevity, Passages North, DIAGRAM, Salon.com, Creative Nonfiction, AGNI, Fourth Genre, Colorado Review, The Pinch*, and many others. He's a founding editor of the literary magazine, *The Normal School*, and teaches in the MFA Program at Fresno State.

Penny Guisinger

Penny Guisinger's work has appeared or is forthcoming in *Fourth Genre, Solstice, Under the Gum Tree*, and others. She holds an MFA from Stonecoast at the University of Southern Maine. She's a Libra (moon in Aries) and an ENFP, who loves sailing, drinking coffee, and that moment just before sleep. Penny lives with her wife, Kara, and the two smartest, most well-read children on earth, Abby and Owen, at the very tip of easternmost Maine.

Michelle Herman

Michelle Herman's most recent book is *Stories We Tell Ourselves*, essays about the unconscious in everyday life. She directs the MFA program in creative writing at Ohio State.

Keith Lesmeister

Keith Lesmeister lives and works in northeast Iowa where he and his family have recently planted an apple and pear orchard. He is an MFA candidate at the Bennington Writing Seminars. This is his first published essay.

Joe Mackall

Joe Mackall is the author of *Plain Secrets: An Outsider Among the Amish*, and of the memoir, *The Last Street Before Cleveland*. He is co-founder and -editor of *River Teeth: A Journal of Nonfiction Narrative*. His work has appeared in many publications, including *The New York Times, The Washington Post*, as well as on National Public Radio's "Morning Edition." He's director of Creative Writing at Ashland University. "Reflections of a Moderately Disturbed Grandfather" is from a memoir in progress, tentatively titled, *Grandparents in Paradise: Life in the Face of the Fall.*

Brenda Miller

Brenda Miller is the author of three essay collections: *Listening Against the Stone* (Skinner House Books, 2012), *Blessing of the Animals* (Eastern Washington University Press, 2009), and *Season of the Body* (Sarabande Books, 2002). She has also co-authored *Tell It Slant: Creating, Refining and Publishing Creative Nonfiction* (McGraw Hill, 2012) and *The Pen and The Bell: Mindful Writing in a Busy World* (Skinner House Books, 2012). Her work has received six Pushcart Prizes. She is a Professor of English at Western Washington University and serves as Editor-in-Chief of the *Bellingham Review*. Her website is www.brendamillerwriter.com.

Leila Philip

Leila Philip is the author of three books of nonfiction, including the award-winning memoir, *A Family Place: A Hudson Valley Farm, Three Centuries, Five Wars, One Family* (Viking 2001, Penguin 2002, SUNY Excelsior 2009). She has received numerous awards from her writing including: the Pen Martha Albrand Citation for Nonfiction and fellowships from the National Endowment for the Arts, The National Endowment for the Humanities, the Radcliffe Research and Study Center, and most recently, the Guggenheim Foundation. "Water Rising" is the title piece of a collaborative project of text and image which counterparts 11 watercolors by artist Garth Evans, with 11 pieces of Philip's writing. The book *Water Rising*, is forthcoming in 2014.

Kim Todd

Kim Todd is the author of *Sparrow; Chrysalis, Maria Sibylla Merian and the Secrets of Metamorphosis*; and *Tinkering with Eden*, a Natural History of Exotic Species in America. Her essays have appeared in *Orion, Sierra, Backpacker*, and *Fourth River*, among other places. She teaches literary nonfiction at Penn State Erie, The Behrend College. "Curious" was written with the help of a residency at the Mesa Refuge.

Nicole Walker

Nicole Walker is the author of the nonfiction book, *Quench Your Thirst with Salt* which won the Zone 3 creative nonfiction prize, released in June 2013, and a collection of poems, *This Noisy Egg* (Barrow Street, 2010). She edited, along with Margot Singer, *Bending Genre: Essays on Nonfiction*, published by Bloomsbury Press in 2013. She has given readings and lectures at The Center for Book Arts in New York City, at Associated Writing Programs in Chicago, New York, and Denver, at NonfictionNow, in Iowa City, as a guest speaker for the Environmental Humanities Conference in Salt Lake City, as an Emerging Writer and at the University of Wyoming. In 2007, she received a fellowship from the National Endowment for the Arts. A graduate of the University of Utah's doctoral program, she is currently Assistant Professor of Poetry and Creative Nonfiction at Northern Arizona University, nonfiction editor of *Diagram* and editor of the artist/writer collaborative project "7 Rings" on the *Huffington Post*.